# Be Good, Do Good

# Be Good, Do Good

*An amateur's guide to making
the world a better place*

## Tom Frist

iUniverse, Inc.
Bloomington

# Be Good, Do Good
## An amateur's guide to making the world a better place

The cover photograph of the earth was taken by NASA.

iUniverse books may be ordered through booksellers or by contacting:

iUniverse
1663 Liberty Drive
Bloomington, IN 47403
www.iuniverse.com
1-800-Authors (1-800-288-4677)

ISBN: 978-1-4620-5755-9 (sc)
ISBN: 978-1-4620-5756-6 (ebk)

Printed in the United States of America

iUniverse rev. date: 10/10/2011

# INDEX

# PART III
## *MAKING THE WORLD*
## *A BETTER PLACE*

# PART IV
## *APPENDIX*

# ENDORSEMENTS

"Once in a great while you come upon a book in which the author takes you with him on a very special journey. And in this case it is not simply a journey that takes you to a strange and exotic land. It is more valuable than that.

Tom Frist invites you to accompany him as he works his own way through the questions that have confirmed the exciting nature of the Christian faith for him. As the two of you walk together, you will find that your own sense of imagination and wonder begins to grow. The long disparaged meaning of goodness in our complex society is rediscovered and becomes a genuine possibility. And you will find that your own valued common sense approach to many things becomes the key to the process.

You follow Frist as he brings his valuable international perspective to bear on the adventure of the Christian faith and you will find, much to your delight, that you have already been launched on a similar journey of your own." **Richard Ray**, former Editor and Managing Director, **John Knox Press**.

"I have known Tom Frist my entire life. No matter where Tom lives or works, his desire is always to lend a helping hand to those in need. This book is written from his heart to yours, with a hope that you will be inspired to go beyond boundaries that may be holding you back from being all you can be in Christ. Tom is no amateur when it comes to inspiring others to 'do good unto all men.'" (Galatians 6:10) **Franklin Graham**, President & CEO, **Billy Graham Evangelistic Association** and **Samaritan's Purse**.

"As founder and president of a non-profit organization that trains younger generation leaders around the world, I have found Tom Frist's book particularly meaningful. Because of our lengthy relationship, I know that he has lived the message of this book. He writes from his varied and quite amazing life of 'being good and doing good.' In his typically thoughtful manner and easy to read style, Tom challenges us with compelling questions and offers practical and useful answers for everyday living. He explores the real issues faced by each one of us as we aspire to become the person we are created to be *from the inside out.* From that perspective, he offers authentic advice on reaching out and doing good to others on both an international level and within our own communities. He allows the reader to introspectively come to his own conclusions about how to 'be good and do good.' This book will cause you to see the world differently and how you can make a difference in it." **Barry St. Clair**, President and Founder, **"Reach Out Youth Solutions."**

"This is a very thoughtful book, lovingly written as a 'how to' for those who wish to share their talents with others. Tom takes the reader on a journey through his mind and heart to examine the reasons for doing good and to explore ways to 'give back' for the good of others. He raises up the possibilities for 'doing good' in individual and global ways. I am reminded of the great call of I Corinthians 12, in which the body of Christ is described as individual members working together for the good of the whole. In Tom's book, he encourages each of us to use our unique, God-given talents, in a diverse panoply of opportunities, to serve out our call 'to do justice, love mercy, and walk humbly.' Tom himself models that call, having given his life to service in a number of ways. He inspires each of us to consider our own calls, blessings, and opportunities." **Bill Scheu**, Chairman of the Board, **Columbia Theological Seminary.**

"From our days at the Presbyterian-related Davidson College to the present when we hike together in the high mountains near Montreat, N.C., where he lives, I have known Tom Frist and witnessed his journey of philosophical and practical faith. Be Good, Do Good is Frist's 21st century restatement of Jesus' answer to the question 'what is God's greatest law?'—Love God with all your heart; love your neighbor as yourself.'

Frist's first novel, <u>The Descendant</u>, was set in a town in Brazil's coffee districts and featured a rehabilitation center for people with Hansen's disease, or leprosy. Frist and his wife, Clare, actually spent much of the 1970s and 1980s in Brazil where he founded SORRI, a national organization of rehabilitation centers for disabled persons, including those affected by leprosy.

From Brazil, Frist was called in the late 1980s to head the American Leprosy Mission, the largest organization combating the disease in the U.S. In 1994, he was elected President of the International Federation of Anti-Leprosy Organizations (ILEP), which fights Leprosy on four continents. A published social scientist, he traveled widely, and now presents this remarkable Christian statement of the reasons for being good (philosophical) and of practical ways of doing it (a virtual how-to). The book beckons to each of us to come to an understanding of our common yearning to live our lives right and particularly shows how individuals actually act on an international plane. Don't miss Appendix II 'A Checklist for Giving,' a second loaf for those who want guidance."
**Hank Ackerman**, former international reporter and bureau chief for **The Associated Press.**

*"I shall pass though this world but once. If therefore there be any kindness I can show or any good thing I can do, let me do it now. For I shall not pass this way again."*
—Stephen Grellet

*"When the Spirit is given to us from heaven, deserts will become orchards thick as fertile forests. Honesty and justice will prosper there, and justice will produce lasting peace and security. You, the LORD's people, will live in peace, calm and secure."*
—Isaiah 32:15-18

# DEDICATION

I dedicate this book to my two children, Lisa Kristin Frist and John Daniel Frist. I hope that it will be helpful to you as you struggle to make sense out of life, to find your gifts and purpose, and to help make the world a better place.

I also dedicate it to the memory of Ruth Bell Graham, a life-long friend, counselor, and beautiful example of what it means to love God, oneself, and others in a practical, compassionate, fun, and joyful way.

# ACKNOWLEDGEMENTS

One of the great joys of life is the realization that people do good to us all of the time. We are all blessed daily by small and large acts of kindness from family, friends, and strangers—those who have gone before us, and those who are with us today. They inspire us with their examples, counsel us with their wisdom, and supply us with our needs.

In the editing of this book in particular, many individuals have helped me, and I want to individually and publically thank them. Among them are my wife Clare, my daughter Lisa, and my brother-in-law Harry Strachan. I also want to thank friends who have taken the time to read the book and to give suggestions or to offer other help. These include John Ackers, Laura Long, Edward Brouwer, Jey Deifell, Ken Abraham, Mark Sweeney, and Eric Nichols.

Those leaders who have read and endorsed the book have done me a great service as well, and I hope that their comments have helped you in your decision to read it.

Finally, I want to thank you, the reader, for taking up this simple account of what it means to one struggling person to live out the two greatest duties of our lives—to love God, and to love others as ourselves. I pray that it will be of help as you, too, seek to make the world a better place.

# INTRODUCTION
## THE STARTING POINT

Some years ago, I came across a poem that I had written to myself as a sophomore on a lazy Sunday afternoon in a Davidson College pine forest. The poem certainly had no literary merit, but the situation it described is one that I find myself in today. In the poem, my college sophomore self imagined my old man self looking back on his life as death approaches and wonders if the old man had fulfilled the dreams of his youth, the dreams that the college sophomore had put on paper.

Now that I have celebrated my 65th birthday, I am approaching the position of the old man in that poem. As I consider my life up until this point, my answer to my sophomore self has to be both "yes" and "no."

I answer "yes" because in many ways, I have led the good life! I have had supportive family and friends with few major personal tragedies. I have experienced good health and basic economic security. I have enjoyed fantastic adventures and have been able to live in many countries in the Americas, in Asia, Europe, and Africa and to travel to many more. I have received splendid educational opportunities in fine institutions and worked in interesting and fruitful jobs in important organizations. In a myriad of ways, my life has been even better and richer than I could ever have imagined some forty-five years ago. I have lived fully and laughed often.

Yet, in other ways, I feel a dismal failure, and my answer has to be a resounding "no!" I have fallen far short of my dreams. It is not that I had grand visions of great fame, wealth, pleasure, and power. I never dreamed in that way. Instead, my deepest yearning was to live my life right.

Of course, like most people, I wanted comfort, pleasure, security, and recognition, but the good life that I wanted was deeper than that. Like Henry David Thoreau, I wanted to "suck out the marrow of life!" I wanted my life to have purpose, to know the good, to be good, and to do good. I wanted to be holy and whole, to have pure motivations, and to act in accordance with them. I wanted to taste the joy that I imagined that such a life would bring. I wanted to advance spiritually, and yes, as pretentious as it sounds, to become a saint. Not one of those flowery or frightening kinds of saints with a pious, dour expression always on their faces, but a wise, true, useful, loving, joyful, and fun saint. I wanted to become a sane person who had seen the light, was transformed by it, and who let that light shine through him to others; a person whose heart of stone had been changed into a spring of living water. I wanted to be good and to do good. I wanted my life to mean something and to play my small part in creating a better world.

## OUR DILEMMA

From my experience, there are many people out there just like me. Maybe you are one of them. We are people who believe that there is meaning and purpose to life and that if we can live our lives in line with that meaning and purpose, then we will fulfill our calling and enjoy lasting happiness. Yet, we fail.

We are people who start out with lofty ideals, but in the harsh reality of living, we find that we are not always able to live up to those ideals.

We want to be good—to be wise, compassionate, and joyful persons, but our insides instead are battlegrounds of warring fears and desires for self-advancement, lustful pleasures, and material comfort.

We want to do good—to relieve suffering where we can and bring beauty, hope, joy, and comfort to those around us. Yet, we fall short because we are hindered by egotism, ignorance, cynicism, and a lack of resources. Instead of the solid and lasting good that we had hoped to accomplish, we find that our achievements are like egotistical chaff blown away by shifting winds.

Problems confront us on every side: poverty, sickness, loneliness, and dishonesty; violence, prejudice, and environmental degradation. We feel overwhelmed by them, and we do not know how to react to them. Our egos tell us that we do not have the wisdom, the resources, or the power to solve them, and therefore our best option is to ignore them and protect our own interests as best we can.

For one living in a developing country, the moral and practical dilemmas one faces are especially acute. When I stop my car at a red light, a child with a pitiful look on his face begs for money. A poorly dressed older girl asks me to buy candy from her. A third boy immediately starts washing my car window with a dirty rag even though, waving him off, I tell him that it was just washed at the last stoplight. On the sidewalk, an amputated war veteran in a dilapidated wheel chair holds up a sign pleading for help. As I drive home through the crowded and trash-strewn streets, a policeman pulls me over for some minor infraction and then suggests that, with a small tip, I can get out of the hassle of going downtown to pay the fine. When I arrive home and am going about my projects, the bell at the gate rings repeatedly, and I go out to talk to someone who tells me that his child needs some medicine, or that his wife has died and needs a coffin, and that he has no money to purchase these things.

Generally, when these sorts of things happen to us, we experience a mixture of emotions from compassion, (because we feel for the person), to incredulity, (because we do not really believe everything that we hear). We also feel guilt that we have so much and the other person has so little, and discomfort because we do not know what to say or do. There is also a sense of self-righteousness and simmering anger at the uninvited intrusion into our lives and at the political system that allows such poverty and corruption to exist. Our main concern is usually to get back as quickly as possible to our own projects and problems.

Those of us who live in more developed countries are also hounded by constant requests for this or that. Panhandlers with their stories of lost wallets and their need for jobs, bus tickets, food, gas, or shelter make us uncomfortable when they approach us. Even more common are the appeals we receive by e-mail, telephone, and snail mail for our financial contributions to a myriad of causes. They ask us to support the church, to cure diseases of all types, to help the disabled, to protect the environment, to provide student scholarships, to give money to the local art museum, to disaster relief, to the local police, or to a political candidate. We also get calls from family and friends who need loans or gifts to help them with their rent or with an upcoming operation or a mission trip. Others ask us to be on this committee or that board, to volunteer for the PTA, or to build houses for the poor.

It is so easy to become hardened and want to say "no" to all of these requests. At the same time we receive the appeal, we are facing our own problems. The stock market is going down, our child wants to attend an expensive school, medical costs are soaring, our car needs fixing, our aging parents need help, and we are worried if we have enough money for our own retirement as we do not want to be a future burden to our children. How can we spare much time and money for others when we have so many personal concerns ourselves?

We also must make important decisions in elections that will influence the good of many. For whom should we vote? Is it better to support a person of good character or one of good sense? A friend who is running for office or a person we do not know personally, but who seems more capable than our friend does? Should we run for office ourselves? What issues should be the most important to us? Should we opt for job creation or for saving the environment, or is there a way to do both even if resources are limited? Should we support the woman's right to choose, or the baby's right to life? What about gay marriage or the traditional values of our religion; the death penalty, or its repeal; military incursions to promote human rights, or non-interference in the affairs of other nations; tax relief, or expanded services for the poor; more foreign aid, or more attention to home issues; tolerance of undocumented immigrants, or insistence on upholding the immigration laws?

All of these questions and many more confront us daily. In many ways, this is a book of questions. What is the good that we should do to others? Why should we do good? Whom should we help? How is it best to help? While the questions are myriad and universal, each of our answers to them must be individual and personal. We yearn for goodness in our hearts and wisdom in our heads to help us answer these questions and to guide us through life.

If you are such a person, then I invite you along on this journey with me to examine possible answers to what it means to be and to do good and how we can get better at it. From the start, you should know that I approach the task of writing about this subject with much trepidation. I am certainly no saint in the sight of my family and friends, and I do not have any special training for discussing this matter. I am neither a theologian-psychologist-ethicist nor an expert in economic development. I am just an amateur deeply aware of my own personal failures who wants to be good and do good better. I write this book mainly to sort through different issues that I have confronted and pondered as I worked in different "do-gooder" organizations in various parts of the world (see pages 85-89). I write it in the hope that thinking through things and putting them on paper will help me grow spiritually and motivate me to be a more productive and less hypocritical doer of good deeds. I write it also because I desire to leave something of myself to my children and their children once I am gone. Despite the book's brevity and simplicity, I hope it will be useful to them and to others whom I have met who have voiced similar dreams and struggles—both the theological and the practical. Maybe you are one of them.

# PART I
## A MAP TO GOODNESS

*"'Love the Lord your God with all your heart and with all your soul and with all your mind. This is the first and greatest commandment. And the second is like it: 'Love your neighbor as yourself.' All the Law and the Prophets hang on these two commandments."*
*(Matthew 22:37-40)*

# CHAPTER 1
## CHOOSING A WORLDVIEW

"Why are we here and how should we live?" These two basic questions have engaged the minds and emotions of humans since people started recording their thoughts. They have also generated a myriad of opposing answers presented in different theories, ideologies, philosophies, and religions.

We all share the same data and we all see and feel the same things—the starry sky stretching out billions of light years, the delicate order in our own bodies and in all of nature. We see beauty and intricate systems everywhere, but we also see ugliness and chaos. We hear laughter, but also weeping; thanksgiving, but also cursing. We rejoice in the birth of a child and then grieve in its inevitable suffering and death. We see people who help others and those who hurt them. A Mother Teresa swirls with a Hitler in our minds.

How do we make sense of all this? How does it all fit together? Is Ultimate Reality—the way things really and finally are—chaos, order, or nothingness? Is the universe ultimately a safe place or a very dangerous one? Is there a Creator, or did everything we see just come about by chance? If there is a Creator, is that Creator good and loving as we know goodness and love, or is that Creator an unfeeling abstract force, or worse yet, hostile? What is our nature as humans? Are we good, evil, or some eternal mixture of both? Do our lives have purpose, or is it all "a tale of sound and fury signifying nothing?" Do we have real choices, or is everything pre-determined by fate?

Evidence exists for all of the above possibilities. Respected philosophers and religious leaders, our fathers and mothers, our teachers and friends, all have their own theories—sometimes radically different one from the other. At times, it seems that we will never know the answers to the questions, and we feel that the only honest position to have is that of the agnostic who says that we do not know and that we cannot know. Our knowledge is so limited. Do not our wisest men like Socrates and Isaac Newton refer constantly to their own ignorance as they try to understand the cosmos? Newton expressed it this way: "I was like a boy playing on the sea-shore, and diverting myself now and then finding a smoother pebble or a prettier shell than ordinary, whilst the great ocean of truth lay all undiscovered before me."

We do not know, but still we all have to interpret the data we have and to live our lives based on some worldview. If we do not, we become lost. Reason can take us only so far. Whatever worldview we choose or whatever action we take, there is in it a component of reason, but also of faith. We drive down the road in faith, believing, but not knowing, that the on-coming car will stay in its own lane. We eat our morning cereal, believing, but not knowing, that a grower, processor, or distributor has not poisoned it. Our entire economic system is based on the faith that everyone will respect the symbolic value of a piece of paper with a number written on it.

In the same way, our interpretation of the cosmos is also an interpretation of faith, founded as much on our fears and desires as on our reason. If we see only a materialistic world created by chance, where the only absolute Truth is that there is no absolute Truth, then that is a vision of faith. If we look around us and see a world created by a moral and loving God, then that, too, is a vision based on our faith.

Our beliefs heavily influence our motivations and our actions. If we believe that the evidence points to an amoral, materialistic world, then we should act in one way. If, on the other hand, we believe in a moral world of order and purpose, then we should act in another. Although this is what should happen, the irony is that some of those who say that we do not live in a moral universe, act morally; while others, who say there is a moral basis to existence, act immorally.

In summary, we all have an internal map or worldview that guides us, whether we are conscious or not of that map. It may be a materialist map based on the faith that what we see is what we get and that all that we see has come about by chance and evolution. It may be a spiritual map based on the faith that the reality that we observe was created and is sustained by a Reality that we cannot see. Some speak of this unseen Reality as a universal Force or Spirit. Others say that this Force or Spirit has a will and personality and they call it God. Some believe in one God and others believe in many. Others even believe that this one God became a man to show us in the flesh what God is like and to redeem us.

I am in the camp of those who believe in this last strange doctrine. While I have lived in many different cultures and studied many different religions and worldviews, I have chosen to call myself a Christian and adopt the Christian worldview as my own. It is therefore the Christian map, as I understand it, which guides me in life and in this book, especially in the first sections. (The main reasons I have committed myself to this view are found in Appendix 1.)

As Christians, we are admonished not only to believe in God with our minds and hearts, but also to do his will with our hands and resources. We are told that by doing his will we promote our ultimate good as well as the good of others. We are enjoined to be and do good since God is Good. Christians believe that being and doing good is the way that we were meant to live, and that it is the roadway to lasting joy for ourselves and for others.

Christianity is not unique in this belief. Other religions and philosophies also teach their followers to be and do good, and many of the followers of these alternate ways lead lives of order and compassion for others that can put many Christians to shame. Yet, there is one basic belief of Christianity that sets Christianity apart in its worldview. This is the concept of Grace. While Christians are admonished to do good, they do not believe that their good deeds are enough to appease God or to "save" them. To the Christian, God's system is not one of "tit for tat." It is one of Grace.

In many other religious systems, salvation is the result of good works. In Christianity, good works are the result of salvation. We love God because he first loved us, and ideally, we do good works as a way of showing our love to him and not out of our fear of his punishment or desire to gain more rewards for ourselves. In fact, Christians are convinced that humans can never be good or holy enough on their own to merit salvation. We need God's intervention and grace for that. Christians believe that such intervention and grace actually happened in the birth, life, teachings, death, and resurrection of Jesus Christ.

Even though knowing that good works cannot save them, Christians are still called to do them. We are constantly admonished in the Bible, by the law, by the prophets, by Jesus, and by Jesus' followers to be and do good. We are constantly pestered by our consciences and by what we call the Spirit of Christ within us to be and do good. Sometimes we do good out of fear of punishment, sometimes out of desire for rewards, but our true deepest wish is to do good out of gratitude, out of love, and in the knowledge that we were created from the beginning to do good works. It is the way that we were made to live. It is the way that we train our children. It is the path to true happiness.

You may believe something different from this. You may want to do good just because you feel it is the way for human beings to live and there is no need to bring a belief in God into it. Maybe you belong to a religion other than Christianity that also teaches you to do good. While I am not one who imagines that all roads lead to the same Truth, as there are critical differences between them, I do believe that God honors the sincere heart that seeks the Truth and is willing to apply the truth that he or she has found. As each of us turns to the light that we have and applies it in our daily lives, I believe that more light is given.

So whatever your worldview and motivation for reading this book, I am honored that you have picked it up. My deepest wish is that it will be useful to you in your attempts to become a better person and a more productive doer of good. We all depend on each other if we are to make the world a better place.

To begin our journey together, let us start with some basic definitions. We say that we want to be and to do good, but what does that mean?

"Good" is one of those words that we all understand, but find hard to put into a concise definition. We know that good is something that is desirable to us or to others. It is something that works the way it is supposed to work, to be what it is supposed to be. Good is used in our language to mean helpful, healthy, attractive, sound, skilled, virtuous, kind, honorable, affording pleasure, among other desirable attributes.

At one level when we talk about good, we mean the supreme "Good," the *Summum Bonum* of the philosophers. This is the highest Good that is eternal, unchanging, and perfect. As Jesus tells us, only God is Good in this way. Therefore, if you believe in God, God's Goodness is the source and the standard for all other good.

At another level when we talk about good, we mean a good that is relative and situational—not eternal. It is a good that can vary by society, person, perspective, time, and circumstance. It is that variableness that makes doing good so difficult for us, as what one person may think is "good" or desirable, another person might think of as "bad" or undesirable. For example, if you win an election or a sports event in which you were competing, that would be a "good" to you. "Good for you, you won!" your supporters might say. Your opponent, however, would classify the same event as "bad" because it was an unwelcomed outcome. "Too bad you lost!"

Even we ourselves may classify something as good one minute and then bad a few minutes later. For example, I crave a banana split, which is good in the sense that it is delicious and fulfills my desires. A little later, after I have eaten it, I bemoan the fact that I have spent my money on the ice cream. Not only do I have less money now for something else, I have broken my diet. The good banana split has become bad to me. The immediate good has become the long-term bad.

Another difficulty that one faces when one tries to choose to do good, is that the choice he or she has to make is not usually between a good and a bad action, but between a good and a better action. Which is the best action for that moment? Do I choose to spend time with my child, to spend the time visiting a sick friend, going to a business meeting, or just reading a book to recharge my batteries? They are all good things to do, but one may be better at that specific time. To choose between good and bad is relatively easy, but it is not so easy to choose between two goods. We are not always sure what criteria to use in our choice.

That is why when we strive for the good in our daily motivations and actions, it is important to be guided by what we consider is the highest Good that we know. For many people, that highest good is their immediate egotistical desires. For others, it might be the good of Humanity—the greatest good for the greatest number of people. For those of us who believe in God, what we perceive as the will of God is our highest Good. Our goal is to bring our own flawed and transitory standards of goodness into line with God's perfect and eternal standard; our own imperfect wills with the perfect will of God. We believe that the day that that happens, we will have become new creatures with new hearts, and the kingdom of God will have come to earth.

This leads us to the question, "How do we know what is the will of God—God's standard of Good?" The answer is that we can only know through God's revelation of himself and of his will. Sometimes that revelation comes to us through nature; sometimes it comes through our reasons evaluating the practical experiences we have had and deciding what works and does not work, and what brings joy and what brings pain. Sometimes the revelation comes from the innate moral sense that seems to be in all men and women; and sometimes it comes through what Christians call the Holy Spirit or the Spirit of Christ within us.

At other times, the revelation of God's will comes through people we call prophets, saints, or mystics—people whom we believe to be inspired by God or messengers of God. They pass on to us in their writings what they claim are God's standards, God's definitions of good, and God's rules for living an abundant life. They tell us how to interpret the events of history and the events of our own lives in the light of these standards. Religious scriptures of all faiths are full of such definitions of what is good and evil and of rules for leading a life pleasing to God. Some of these definitions and rules are temporary and targeted to certain peoples. Others are for all times and for all people. Many of the standards of different religions overlap and lead us therefore to believe that we all share many basic experiences and beliefs in God.

Christians believe, however, that while God reveals himself in many similar ways to all of us, it is through the life, example, and teachings of Jesus Christ that we learn most accurately and completely what is God's nature and will. Jesus claimed that only he had seen God, that he and God were one, and that no one could come to God but by him. While such claims may sound dubious to our reason and offend our democratic inclusive principles, Christians believe that these claims were confirmed by the life, by the miracles, and most of all, by the physical resurrection of Jesus. Thus, the Christian believes that the surest way to live a good and fulfilling life is to follow the example and teachings of Jesus and to allow his spirit to guide us.

## SACRIFICIAL LOVE IS GOD'S STANDARD OF GOOD

It is through Jesus that we learn that sacrificial love is the very nature of God and the way to him. It is God's standard of good and the map to our own inner transformation and to the transformation of the world around us. It is the map that we should follow if we truly wish to be good and do good and make the world a better place.

Jesus makes this clear when he replies to a question asked by an expert in Jewish law as to which of the laws given by God were the most important. In his answer, he said:

*"'Love the Lord your God with all your heart and with all your soul and with all your mind. This is the first and greatest commandment. And the second is like it: 'Love your neighbor as yourself.' All the Law and the Prophets hang on these two commandments."* (Matthew 22:37-40)

Because Jesus gave us these two Old Testament commands to follow, let us now turn our attention to examining what it means to love God, to love ourselves, and to love our neighbors practically. How do we do that? To begin, we will first try to understand what Jesus meant by the word "love."

# CHAPTER 3
## *WHAT IS LOVE?*

Love, like good, is another one of those words that have taken on all kinds of meanings, some of which might even be contradictory to the meaning that Jesus intended for it to have. We say that we love God, we love our country, we love our children, we love ice cream, we love football, we make love, and we call something beautiful or good, lovely. Surely, one word cannot have the same meaning for all of the above situations. They are vastly different in kind and degree. The question is then, what meaning did Jesus have for the word when he used it? Is it an attitude, a feeling, a willing, an action, a force, or all of the above?

I think that it is all of the above, but most of all, it is willing. Usually, when Jesus uses the word love, the writer who records what he says employs the Greek expression *agape* to describe what he meant. What most scholars think that Jesus denoted by *agape* love is an unselfish, unconditional, volitional, active, benevolent, and sacrificial concern for the real and long term good of the beloved. *Agape* love involves will, duty, humility, empathy, kindness, and delight in the other. It involves sacrifice and union. It involves action. It means getting out of oneself and carrying another's burdens. Jesus tells us that in its highest manifestation, *agape* love means to lay down one's life for another, even those who are different from us and who oppose us. This is the love that God has for us. Jesus illustrates this love by freely choosing to die for our good—to be the "sacrificial lamb that takes away the sin of the world."

*Agape* love is the highest, most spiritual of the loves, distinguished in degree from *philia*—the affection of friendship, and *eros*—sexual love. As Paul describes it in Corinthians, *agape* love is the ultimate virtue that contains all the other virtues. *Agape* love is patient and kind;

it does not envy or boast; it is not arrogant or rude; it does not insist on its own way; it is not irritable or resentful; it does not rejoice in doing wrong, but rejoices in the truth. It bears all things, believes all things, hopes all things, and endures all things. It is eternal.

*Agape* love is both the source of goodness and the goal of goodness. It is the greatest value for which we can strive and the force that moves us towards the goal. It is the *Summum Bonum,* the supreme Good. A vision of this Good is a vision of God. Even popular culture agrees with that, as can be seen by the title of John Lennon's song "All You Need is Love." Since God is defined in the Bible as Love, loving God means in one sense that we are to love Love.

All religions and self-improvement books are full of rules and admonitions written to help guide us to happiness and success as we pass through life. They tell us how to get along with each other and thus lead a secure and happy life. Jesus tells us that Love is the fulfilling of all of these rules. Love is the one thing that we must learn to do. If you love someone, you have that person's good in your mind, in your heart, and in your soul. You would never want to hurt them, but only to do them good. You would not murder them, steal from them, rape them, fool them, or slander them. Instead, you would seek out ways to serve them. Love thus simplifies life and all of the other rules.

Another wonderful thing about *agape* love is that it not only simplifies things, it is contagious. When you give love to others, others most often want to give it back to you and even "pass it on," sharing it with still others. When we know that God loves us, we want to love God and all of his creation in return.

Still, even though the spark of love is in us naturally, we have to do our best to blow on it to fan and kindle it, so that it grows into a great flame that will bring honor to God, as well as light, warmth, and happiness to ourselves and to others. We must try to learn for ourselves what it means to love God, to love ourselves, and to love others in the right way. Then we must try to put what we have learned into practice, doing the good works that we have been called to do.

This is the subject matter of the following chapters—trying to be good and do good by loving in the right way. It is important to remember, however, that we can only advance so far on our own. Without humility and God's grace, we will surely fail in our efforts. We can do our best to learn, to will, and to obey, but in the final analysis, only God can transform our minds, our wills, and our hearts, and make us and our world into what we were meant to be.

# CHAPTER 4
## *WHAT DOES IT MEAN TO LOVE GOD?*

I think that I have always believed in a Creator God, mainly because I cannot imagine how such a complex and beautiful world could come about without a Designer, Creator, and Sustainer. It has always seemed so unscientific and unreasonable to me to believe that all we see just came about by chance, even given the enormous amounts of time we give for it to happen. Yet, more and more intelligent people today believe just that.

Whether we believe in God or not, we all believe that there is an Ultimate Reality—the way things really are. We just do not know the nature of this Ultimate Reality. Whatever it is—Chaos, Change, Order, Energy, Matter, Spirit, or Nothingness—this Ultimate Reality exists on its own, no matter what our theories, philosophies, and religions might conceive it to be. It is the Truth because it is what is. It is the Good because it is the Truth.

I believe there are two basic methodologies that men and women use to deal with their questions concerning Ultimate Reality. One is the methodology of the scientist and the other is the methodology of the theologian. Both the scientist and theologian use observation, reason, and different levels of faith to arrive at their conclusions about the nature of Ultimate Reality.

The scientist seeks to understand the cosmos by investigating its material make-up, its cause, and the relationship of the material things within it. The scientist observes, comes up with theories, creates experiments to test those theories, and uses logic to interpret the results. The conclusions that the scientist reaches must be tested and corroborated by other scientists before being considered true. In science, truth is a relative term and not an absolute one. New data is always coming in that challenge past conclusions. Thus, our scientific ideas of the universe's beginnings, basic building blocks, direction, and end are constantly changing. Whether or not this change brings us closer or takes us further away from the correct understanding of the way things really are—Ultimate Reality—we of course do not know yet. The conclusions of the scientist are therefore conclusions of faith, "based on the best available evidence."

While scientists limit themselves to the study of the material world and of things that can be measured and tested, theologians believe that there is more to reality than just those things that we can now see and measure with our senses and instruments. There are mysteries beyond our human capacities to unveil. One of the main tools theologians use for understanding this unseen and mysterious world is revelation, which we talked about some in chapter two.

Revelation happens in different ways. It sometimes happens directly to us, and in an *eureka* moment, everything comes together and makes sense. We obtain a glimpse of the real nature of things or of Ultimate Reality by grace. We can prepare for this moment, but we cannot force it. Such a moment happened to Blaise Pascal and Thomas Aquinas.

Pascal was a brilliant mathematician and scientist, who in his head knowledge invented calculus and the mechanical calculator. Yet, he was also a mystic who experienced God in a moment of insight that changed his life. His experiential knowledge trumped his head knowledge, and he came to orient the rest of his life around the heart knowledge of the mystic, rather than the head knowledge of the scientist. As he writes in his notes, "The heart has its reasons that reason knows not of."

Saint Thomas Aquinas was a theologian and considered by many as one of the most intelligent men who ever existed. He also had a momentary vision of Ultimate Reality that he said made all his numerous volumes of rational theology seem as straw. This moment of grace and insight trumped all his years of tedious reasoning.

I have never had such a life transforming revelation of Ultimate Reality. Yes, I personally have experienced moments of deep peace, comfort, and sudden insights, but I've never had what I would call a mystic experience in which everything fell into place—where total understanding and assurance enveloped me. I wish so much that I had. Would it not be wonderful if we were able to see Ultimate Reality with clear vision and not have to struggle as a scientist, as a theologian, or as a normal human being with so many unanswered questions, doubts, and fears?

Since most of us, I believe, are in the same boat, we depend for our conception of Ultimate Reality on others whom I will call Truth-tellers. Some of us choose to stick with the Truth-tellers who espouse only scientific theories and explanations of the moment as to the nature of our cosmos. Others of us are willing to listen also to the prophets and the mystics who claim that they have had a glimpse of Ultimate Reality and have shared what they have experienced with the rest of us. Of course, we have to use our reason to determine if these people really are reliable Truth-tellers or if they are just charlatans or crazy persons. I have seen my share of all three and realize that there are many unstable people and even scoundrels or who claim such visions. They, however, cannot back up their claims by their character, by supporting signs, or by reason.

Truth-tellers are deemed reliable if what they say makes sense, is supported by other Truth-tellers, and comes true. We believe them if what they say is backed up by personal character and by extraordinary signs such as miracles. Just as scientists test materialistic theories, we also must test what mystics and prophets claim they have seen and heard. If after examination, they are seen to be worthy of trust and their experiences of Ultimate Reality are deemed to be true, then their teachings are listened to. Sometimes their teachings even become accepted as infallible scriptures.

This is what happened with Moses. Moses told the Israelites in Egypt that he had heard the voice of God in the desert telling him that he was to go back to Egypt to free them from slavery, to lead them to Mount Sinai to worship God and receive his commandments, and eventually to guide them to the Promised Land. This voice that spoke to Moses uses the name "I AM" to identify himself and thus states that he is Ultimate Reality. He also used a perpetually burning bush and a miracle staff that turned into a serpent as signs to Moses that truly it was God who was speaking to him. Moses then used this staff and other signs provided to him by "I AM" to convince the Israelites that he had indeed heard God's voice and commands, and that God had chosen him to be his spokesperson.

While the Christian venerates Moses as a legitimate Truth-teller, they look beyond him and other prophets to Jesus as the ultimate Truth-teller. Christians believe that Jesus Christ is much greater than even Moses, and has not only taught us the truth about Ultimate Reality, but that he is in fact the physical manifestation of Ultimate Reality. Jesus uses the same name of the Deity, "I AM," to apply to himself (John 8:58), and he claims to be the Truth in his statement "I am the way, and the truth, and the life." (John 14:6) He also says that he and God are one in a unique sense. Said to be without sin by his disciples, Jesus is viewed as the ultimate standard of Good by Christians. Before Jesus leaves his followers as a physical presence, he tells them that he will never forsake them and that he will be with them in Spirit and will continue to guide them into truth and goodness.

Because of such Truth-tellers as Moses and Jesus, Christians believe in a personal and benevolent Ultimate Reality. Christians call this Ultimate Reality by many names—I AM, God, Yahweh, the Lord, the Almighty, the Eternal, Heavenly Father, are just a few of them. Most of these names connote that Ultimate Reality is not just some impersonal concept like Truth, Good, Love, or Beauty or some impersonal force like Nature, but a Spirit with personality, will, and purpose, all of which are holy and good.

The basic message we have received from Moses, the prophets, and especially from Jesus and his trusted followers, is that this Spirit created us and loves us as a good father loves his child. Jesus gives us the beautiful and comforting parable of the return of the prodigal son as an example of this love. Like the best earthly father, God wants only our ultimate good and he is always there to provide for us, teach us, discipline us, pick us up, forgive us, and encourage us. Our task as sons and daughters is to focus all of our thoughts and feelings and actions

23

on him—to acknowledge with thankfulness and awe his existence and power, to accept his wisdom, to trust his goodness and love for us, and to follow his directions as the standard for our lives. That is what the command "to love God with all of our heart, soul, and mind" means to me.

Loving God with all our heart, soul, and mind means also that we are to have a passion for God. A story that illustrates this passion is told in a number of religious traditions. A young disciple asks his teacher how it is possible as a creature to see and know God. Before he answers, the teacher takes the young man to a river and holds his head under the water until his lungs are about to burst. Finally, the teacher lets the struggling young man up to fill his gasping lungs with precious air. Only then does the teacher answer the youth. "You will see and know God once your desire for him is as great as your desire was for air when I held your head under water." Unfortunately, most of us lack that passionate love for God that both Moses and Jesus claimed was the greatest need for our lives.

# CHAPTER 5
## *HOW CAN WE LEARN TO LOVE GOD?*

So what do we do? To love God in that passionate and total way is a tall order for most of us. First, it is hard because some of us have trouble believing in a Creator and Personal God as Ultimate Reality. Some of us feel that science can explain most of our life here, except of course, for "the big bang" that set it and evolution into motion.

A second reason why we struggle to love God is that we are confused as to his nature and ways. The world he created is full of order, beauty, and goodness, but it is also full of chaos, evil, and suffering. The Bible, the Koran, and other scriptures picture God as Just, Loving, and Merciful to all humanity, but also from time to time, they show him as ordering the slaughter of women and children in this world, showing favoritism to particular people, and condemning unbelievers to an eternal hell of terrible suffering in the world to come. This mixed portrayal of God perplexes us morally and fills us with fear.

While the presence of suffering in the world has always been a source of doubt and skepticism about God, the concept of an everlasting hell is even more difficult to understand. How can an all powerful and all good God allow such things?

Many of us can understand a purgatory sort of hell where punishment is limited in time and scope with the end goal of purging us of our impurities. God is a like a loving parent who disciplines us so that we will grow up into decent human beings.

We can also understand a hell that we choose for ourselves. Our egos do not usually enjoy living under the rule of someone better or greater than we are, and we do not like to be around certain types of people. Therefore, we can understand someone choosing what they consider personal freedom even over the joy of heaven. Is that not what Satan's choice was?

Yet, what is hard to understand and accept is an eternal hell of incredible pain whose only purpose is to quarantine and punish unbelievers. How could anyone in heaven, our brothers and sisters, our parents and friends, much less God our Heavenly Father, be anything but miserable knowing that their loved ones were in such a hell? Nor can we understand how a loving God, who wants all people to be saved, could predestine the vast majority of humanity to such a place. For many of us, this latter type of hell just does not fit in with the concepts of God's goodness, love, mercy and fatherhood that are the basis of the entire Christian message. It also does not fit in with the belief that God is in total control of the cosmos.

A third reason some of us struggle to love God as Jesus taught is that we are not quite sure what to make of Jesus and the Christian claim that he is the way, the truth, and the life, and that no one comes to God but by him. At one level of our brain, it defies belief that a poor carpenter living over 2,000 years ago in an obscure part of the world, did great miracles and then died a horrible death that somehow was necessary for the salvation and good of all persons. We find it hard to grasp that soon after this violent death, he came back to life, showed himself physically to many, and today lives in the hearts of his followers. Most of all we do not know how to deal with the claim that this human Jesus, is God himself, the Creator and Sustainer of the cosmos. We are willing to accept Jesus as a good man, a wise teacher, a prophet, a son of God among many sons of God as in other Eastern religions, but it is quite another decision to accept him as uniquely, the very image and substance of God himself.

A fourth reason some of us cannot love God with all our heart, soul, and mind are our strong egos. We do not like to accept the idea that we are subject to a higher authority or that the universe does not revolve around our own personal understanding, needs, and wants. Believing and loving God in that way means that all of our personal pride and desires become secondary. Loving God with all our hearts, souls, and minds means that everything revolves around God and not us, and we are not sure that we like that!

If we have any such questions and doubts, how is it possible to love God with all of our being? A father, when asked by Jesus if he believed that Jesus had the power to cure his child, answered, "I do believe; help me to overcome my unbelief!" (Mark 9:24) Many of us can identify with that father. We can only believe so much by our own strength.

It may be that we can believe in a Creator God and we can believe that Jesus by his life, teachings, claims, miracles, and resurrection is the human who most mirrors who God is. Still part of us remains skeptical, and we cannot believe with all of our heart, soul, and mind.

It may be that we believe that God is good, loving, and merciful because of what scriptures say, because of what Jesus did, and because what our own life experiences confirm. Yet, we also know that suffering abounds, and that we ourselves, and most of those whom we know, are huge failures when measured by God's standards of goodness. Therefore, a part of us remains fearful, as we know that God, who is holy, has the power to take our life and cast our soul into hell. Scripture says that the fear of God is the beginning of wisdom, but it also says that perfect love casts out all fear. Since our love is yet imperfect, our fears remain. It is very difficult to love with all our heart, soul, and mind someone or something we fear.

We therefore believe, but with reservations. We cannot force ourselves to believe something that we do not actually think is true, or love something that we do not think is good. We can *want* to believe and to love, and we can *will* to believe and to love, but we can only *totally* believe and love when reason, experience, and love convince us.

So for those of us who believe in and love God a little, but not yet with all of our heart, soul, and mind, what then can we do besides wait for God to transform us by an *eureka* moment? Here are some things we might consider:

**We can be honest.** If God is Truth, then obviously he wants us to be honest with ourselves, with others, and with him. Anyway, it is impossible to fool God!

One of the most attractive things about the Bible for me is that it shows people as they are with all of their warts, doubts, and weaknesses. There is no hiding of defects! Abraham, the friend of God, is a coward and a deceiver at times. Jacob is a false schemer. Moses, who speaks with God directly, is a murderer, speaks imperfectly, and has moments of frustration and pride. Job and Jeremiah often argue with and complain to God; and David, the glorious king and psalmist, is a scheming, adulterous murderer. The "Chosen People" of God constantly fail him and the disciples of Jesus run away and doubt him. One of my favorite books of the Bible is Ecclesiastes, written by Solomon, the wisest of kings and an honest person, but also a man with many major defects. That this skeptical book and all of the stories of the failings of people who are supposedly heroes made it into the Bible, says something about God's love for Truth as well as about his Mercy. That is so liberating! We are all like the Biblical heroes—sinful, egotistical, and struggling humans, yet capable of being loved by God and of loving him in return.

**We can seek.** All through the Bible, we are told to seek God and his righteousness. *"Seek the Lord while he may be found."* (Isaiah 55:6) *"You will seek me and find me when you seek me with all your heart."* (Jeremiah 29:13) *"Seek first his kingdom and his righteousness and all these things will be given to you as well."* (Matthew 6:33)

My advice to anyone who does not believe in a Personal God is to seek what is the highest and best that you can think of—Truth, Goodness, Joy, Enlightenment. Turn your head and walk toward the brightest and purest light that you have right now. That light is a glimmer of who God is. We have the promise and the hope that while we are seeking God, that he is seeking us. When we have found him or been found by him, we have acquired the pearl of great price for which we would sell all. If we have eyes to see, we can see God all around us:

We can see him in nature. Seek him therefore in the forests and mountains, gardens, oceans, streams, and air. One of the most beautiful books I have ever read is Thomas Traherne's Centuries of Meditation, in which page after page speaks of the imprint of God in nature. John Donne and other poets also see nature as a library full of images showing the mark and purpose of God. Jesus used images of nature—of flowers in the field, birds in the air, fig trees, spouting seeds, vines of grapes, and many more to illustrate what the kingdom of God is like. So look for God in both the thunder and in the silence of nature, in its intricate design and miraculous abundance, beauty, balance, and renewal.

Science is a valuable tool to help us look at nature and discover the blueprints and imprint of God. Remember, throughout history, far more scientists have been believers in God than not. Christianity is a religion that values truth, and it values the material world created by God and declared good by him. True science is the believer's friend rather than enemy.

We can seek God in history. We can see God in the lives and stories of so many who have gone before us. We can see the evil that he hates and the good that he loves. We can see him in the history of our own communities, families, and organizations, and in the faith, sacrifice, and good deeds of God lovers. Some say that the history of the Jewish people is one of the proofs of the existence of God. That this small, obscure tribe of people has survived despite so many persecutions and has had such an astounding impact on the history of the world in religion, literature, and science, is a miracle in itself. Israel has undergone total devastation in its homeland, confronted exile and scattering around the world, experienced segregation, and of course the holocaust. Yet, with all its faults, it remains as a witness to God.

We can seek God in art, in music, in literature, and in philosophy. Humans hunger for purpose, for the Good, the Beautiful, and the True, and artists fill their creative works with this longing. Bach, Michelangelo, John of the Cross, Aquinas, Donne, are just a tiny example of all the myriad of men and women who raise our thoughts and spirits to higher levels because of their inspired creations. Their yearning, inspiration, and ability to create such glorious masterpieces come from somewhere. Many would say they emanate from God, the first Creator. Bach always signed his pieces, "Soli Deo Gloria—to the Glory of God alone."

We can seek God in Jesus Christ. For Christians, and even people of some other religions, Jesus Christ is a concrete and historical revelation of the invisible God. He reflects God's sacrificial love for us. In him, we see God's wisdom, God's goodness, and God's power over disease, nature, and even death. Jesus tells us about and shows us concretely the nature of God. He instructs us in how we should live, and he gives us hope and encouragement. Because of Christ, we know that Good, Truth, and Life will triumph over evil, falsehood, and death. Because of him, we also know that we as individuals matter to God who loves us.

We can seek God in others. Not only successful people show us the face of God, but so can the poor, the helpless, and the outcasts. Jesus said that when we help them, we are helping him. *"Whatever you did for one of the least of these brothers and sisters of mine, you did for me."* (Matthew 25:40) Mother Teresa was famous for saying that she saw the face of God in the faces of the poorest of the poor whom she served.

With humility and discernment, we can see the face of God in everyone. We can see him in the erudite, who seek God in learning and reason; in the devout, who seek God in worship; in the prophetic, who warn us of the dangers in our immoral ways of living; in the compassionate, who seek him in service; in the humble, who allow themselves to be served. We can seek God in friends and family and in other believers, sharing with them our struggles and hopes. We can even seek God in those outside our own religious tradition who seek God wholeheartedly. Even though we may believe in the marrow of our bones that the Christian way is Truth, we also know that God shows himself to and honors all seekers who have sincere hearts. We are all creatures of the same God and brothers and sisters under the same Father.

We can even seek God in ourselves. Jesus said that the kingdom of God is within us, so that is where we should seek him. What a vast and complicated world we have within us, full of despair and hope, of weakness and strength, of evil and good, and of so many conflicting desires. We need to be attentive to that world—to the complexities of our bodies, emotions, and minds. We need to know our inner yearning for goodness and truth, but also our propensities for manipulation, falseness, and hypocrisy. We need to listen carefully to our desires, our dreams, our thoughts, our inner moral code, and to God's still small voice within us. Silent meditation each day is a useful practice to calm our spirits, sharpen our understanding, and deepen our compassion.

Even though we can seek and find evidence of God in all of these things, we must also remember that as creatures, we will never be able to see God fully. Our eyesight and minds are too feeble, and God's nature, power, wisdom, holiness, and love are so far beyond all that we can imagine or think. We are like ants trying to understand calculus. We must make the leap of faith when the light we have only shines so far.

**We can read scripture with the careful spirit of someone who wants to learn, understand, and obey.** The Bible is considered a book from God, not only by Christians and Jews, but by others as well. Christians believe that the Old and New Testaments of the Bible are the source of most of what we know about God—about his being, character, purpose, and actions among men. To advance in holiness and goodness, we must therefore study and meditate on scripture systematically, not only with our heads, but also with our hearts. In the Bible, we learn not only of the history, struggles, failings and triumphs of others who sought to know God, but we also gain insight into ourselves. Just as parents gradually guide their children into a responsible adulthood, so does God lead us to a higher understanding of our roles in the world through the pages of the Bible.

**We can pray.** Prayer is communicating with God, sometimes with our mouth, sometimes with our silent yearnings, but always with our inner ears and heart. Prayer is the foundation of the life of faith. It is also one of its greatest paradoxes. How can it be that God, who knows everything about us and who is an eternity beyond us in nature and holiness, wants us to talk with him and to hear him? Why should we pray, unceasingly as the Apostle Paul says?

The answer is that we should pray to learn the will of God and to align our will and actions to his. We pray in order to seek, to delight in, and submit ourselves to Ultimate Goodness, Truth, and Beauty. We pray in order to praise and to be thankful for life and for all the good things that we have and experience daily. We pray to listen. We pray in desperation for our own needs and for the needs of others. We pray to seek mercy and forgiveness for our countless failures, and we pray for strength, desire, and wisdom so that we can be God's hands in the world helping to bring in his kingdom. We pray to be in his presence, for we are told that in his presence is fullness of joy. We pray that all men and women will one day come to know him and that his kingdom of peace and love be ushered in. Prayer is ultimately important because it takes us out of our superficial selves and into our deepest selves where we can sometimes hear the voice of God.

**We can obey.** It does us no lasting good if all of our lives we are only seekers and not doers of God's will. Loving God totally means making his will our own. We must apply what we have learned. Mark Twain once said, "It is not the parts of the Bible that I cannot understand that bother me, it's the parts that I do understand." Even if the light we see in front of us to guide us is very dim, we need to walk towards it with faith that as we get closer to it, that light will become brighter and brighter.

The reality is that we really do not know something until we actually practice it. We all have different talents and tasks to do. Jesus promises us that if we are faithful in our use of our talents to do the tasks that we have been given, more will be given to us. In this way, we will be constantly advancing in knowledge and wisdom and in our love for God and man. We will become more Christ-like and more efficient servants.

**We can trust.** Trust is fundamental to seeking, to prayer, to obedience, and to love. We must trust that we can actually connect with the God whom we seek and that we can confide in him. We can trust because the Bible tells us that God loves us and we can actually see this love in the mercies and kindnesses of our lives. We just need to look around us in order to become aware of how much good in life is provided to us free of charge—air, water, plants growing, beauty, warm sunshine, soft breezes, the love of parents, daily acts of kindness, and words of encouragement and comfort. We can see how much others help us by providing for our food, clothes, entertainment, safety, and learning.

The more convinced that we are of God's love for us and that he only wants our good, the more we will love him and will want to do his will. Similarly, the more convinced we are that God is all wise, all true, all good, and all powerful, the more we will trust him with the direction of our lives and the lives of the people we love. If he really is God, then he knows a lot more than we do! With trust, we become like little children submitting to the provision and directions of a loving parent. With trust, even when we do not totally understand, we can say along with Julian of Norwich, "all shall be well, all shall be well, and all manner of things shall be well." When we believe and trust like that, then we will finally be able to love God our Creator, Sustainer, Lord, Teacher, Redeemer, Father, and Friend with all of our heart, soul, and mind.

In summary, loving God with all one's heart, soul, and mind is the very basis of any good that we are or can do. It is so much easier to be and do good, if first, we are convinced that God exists and that he is all powerful and good; that he loves us and wants our good; and that he is present to guide and strengthen us in our efforts to be and do good. It is also easier to do good if we are convinced that in the end, Love and the Good will win out both in our own lives and in all of creation. Yes, like all competing views of Ultimate Reality, the Christian view requires a leap of faith, but it is a leap based on reasonable hope and solid evidence.

# CHAPTER 6
## *What does it mean to love ourselves?*

In one sense, I am glad that Jesus included the phrase, "as yourself" when he said that "you should love your neighbor as yourself." I may have a hard time loving God and my neighbor, but I have no trouble whatsoever with loving myself! I can do that without a commandment. I imagine that you might sigh in relief as well.

Yet, that being said, isn't "loving ourselves" in contradiction with other sayings of Jesus and those of his followers that suggest that we should deny ourselves, think of others as better than ourselves, and even crucify ourselves? In fact, the death of self is one of the main tenets of Christianity. Jesus tells us that there can be no resurrection of a new self, if the old self has not first died. *"Unless a kernel of wheat falls to the ground and dies, it remains only a single seed. But if it dies, it produces many seeds."* (John 12:24) Are these commands then to love oneself and to die to oneself a contradiction, or are they another one of those Christian paradoxes?

## *Many selves within us*

I think they are one of those Christian paradoxes. The truth is that we have many selves within us. Some we should love, and some we should crucify. Even the statement, "I love myself," confirms the multiplicity of selves. In this simple declaration, the self that loves, "I," is different from the self that is loved, "myself." We can classify these interior selves in many different ways. Perhaps the most familiar to us are the "mind, soul, and spirit" of the Greek philosophers, or Freud's "ego, id, and super-ego." Besides these selves of the philosophers and psychologists, we all know that in our own lives we put on different

34

selves for different circumstances. Our child self is different from our parent self which is also different from our spouse and professional selves, just to name a few of the legion of selves that we have within us.

My own experience in thinking about who I am is that I have at least four primary selves within me along with many other smaller selves. Three of these selves are at constant war with each other, and the fourth serves as a referee between them. It makes the final decision as to what to will and how to act.

One of my warring selves, I call my <u>Dark self.</u> It shows itself from time to time by seeping into my consciousness as despair, apathy, or egotistical pride. Sometimes it bursts in and attempts to control my mind and body as anger, hate, lust, and fear. The Dark self knows no reason or order, no kindness or empathy. It is thoughtless, raw emotion. Sometimes it acts on its own; sometimes it is allied with other dark forces from without. The Christian would call these external forces Satan and his spirits.

A second major self, I call my <u>Yearning self</u>. This self longs for the Good and for the Beautiful, for the deepest Truth and Joy, and for meaning and purpose in life. It dominates late at night or in the early morning when all is quiet and I am alone in meditation. It speaks to me on a hike when I contemplate some magnificent scene in nature, smell the first drops of rain in the dust, or refresh myself with water and a delicious rest after a hard climb. This Yearning self believes that the cosmos and my life have meaning and purpose. It says that a loving Creator made all of the marvelous things that we see—the tiny insects and the giant galaxies, the complicated eye that sees and the ear that hears. It believes that there is a way of holy and good living that fits the design, and a way of living that does not. If we follow the good way, we will experience the joy that comes from having our lives in harmony with Ultimate Reality—the way things really are and should be. It yearns to know good, to be good, to do good, and for union with the Good. It is peaceful, thankful, and compassionate and sees others as brothers and sisters, and is willing to sacrifice itself for them. It believes that there is a kingdom of God within us and that one day there will be a kingdom of God outside of us too when all shall be well. This self seems to be the self with whom God's spirit most often chooses to communicate.

Then there is my <u>Skeptical self</u>. It takes over in the midst of crowds and noise, of wheeling and dealing, of ambition for power, position, and wealth. It describes itself in terms like "practical" and "realistic" and mocks my Yearning self as ignorant, naïve, and full of fantasy. Death and oblivion, it says, is our only end and self-interest is our only motor. To be happy, we should therefore grab as many toys, positions, accolades, accomplishments, pleasures, and experiences as we can before we die. As the saying goes, "He who dies with the most toys, wins!" My Skeptical self often justifies and sometimes allies itself with my Dark self. If we must fool others to get what we want, that is all right. After all, they are out to get the same playthings that we want, and they will manipulate us to get them if we let them. My Skeptical self urges me to see others as objects and competitors and to employ manipulation and even some degree of deceit in getting what I want. It puts down others in order for it to look superior.

Besides these three warring selves that push their opposite visions and agendas, I have a fourth self inside of me, which I call my <u>Deciding Self</u>. It is the one that hears the arguments from Dark, Yearning, and Skeptical, considers their desires and evidence, and then decides how to believe and act. My Deciding Self, I believe, is my fundamental Self, the Self of my own individuality, will, and destiny. It is who I really am. Sometime my Deciding Self favors the Dark self, sometimes the Skeptical, and sometimes the Yearning self. Sometimes it is unable to choose. Always, though, it bases its decisions and actions on a mixture of reason, emotion, and of faith.

My Deciding Self is writing this book after it has listened to my other three selves. It hears the deep whisper of the Yearning self that beckons us to trust, to love, to share; that encourages us to strive for the goal of goodness on a personal level and the kingdom of God on the social. It hears also the more shrill voices of the Dark and Skeptical selves that mock such aspirations as ludicrous, hypocritical, and impractical. Instead, those voices say, what really matters is immediate pleasure, looking out for number one, and accumulating and protecting what is rightfully ours.

Many religious persons, such as Hindus and Buddhists, believe that all of the inner selves that I have described are illusions. According to them, we have only one true Self that the Hindus call "Atman." This Self is the individual manifestation of the universal God Brahman. When we finish peeling through all the layers of illusions and peripheral selves and external spirits speaking within, the Atman is the only reality that remains. It is the same as the universal God.

The Christian would never say that God and one's fundamental self are the same, but the Christian does believe that the transcendent God in the form of the Holy Spirit lives within the Christian, giving comfort and direction. The final goal of the Christian is to become aware of and then to become one with the Spirit of God within us. Not one in substance of course, for that is impossible since we are creatures and not the Creator, but one in will and purpose. In the ideal Christian life, the Deciding Self is able to distinguish the voice of the Holy Spirit within us, and chooses to follow the directions of that voice. When that happens, as Paul the Apostle said, *"I no longer live, but Christ lives in me."* (Galatians 2:20)

## PURGATION AND UNION: CHOOSING THE HIGHER OVER THE LOWER

"Loving ourselves" in the Christian sense means that we decide to follow the leadings of the voice of Christ within us, to become branches to Christ's vine. It means rejecting evil and choosing the best over the good and choosing lasting joy over momentary pleasures.

We all want happiness, but we seek it in different places. Some of us search for it mainly in basic sensual pleasures such as food, sex, and comfort. Some of us look for it in wealth and power, because we feel that these will give us access to sensual pleasures and the freedom to do as we please. Some of us also seek happiness in the praise of others that affirms us and sets us apart from them.

All of these do bring a type of happiness. Sensual pleasures like sex and gourmet eating do bring delight. The same is true of spiritual pleasures like being praised or enjoying the beauty of nature, art, music, children, and so many other lovely things around us. These are all great gifts of God and reveal to us the goodness of his creation. Yet, because these pleasures are so ephemeral, they can also bring us great pain when they disappear because of sickness, boredom, aging, fickleness, and death.

Wealth gives us pleasure because it allows us freedom and opportunities to please ourselves and others. Yet, it also brings us pain and worries about thieves, taxes, stock market crashes, fires, legal suits, and so on. Power, like wealth, is an excellent tool for doing good, but as an end in itself, it can blind and bind us. We always want just a little bit more of it, and sometimes we even abandon our own moral codes to preserve what we have. We eye with suspicion those who would try to take away from us the little power that we have, or keep us from getting more.

Saints also seek happiness, but they seek it primarily in the alignment of their will and of their actions with that which they understand is the will of God. They turn their faces towards the light that they see and cooperate as best they can with the voice of the Holy Spirit within them. Their happiness is in knowing that they are cooperating with the Good Master, and their greatest desire is to hear the words *"well done, good and faithful servant . . . come and share your master's happiness."* (Matthew 25:21) They believe, with all of their hearts, Dante Alighieri's statement that *"In His will is our peace."* They crave for the Spirit of God to empty them of anything that hinders them from advancing towards this highest happiness.

Earthly pleasures are good, but the religious person knows that we should place them under the authority of God who is the source of both our life and happiness. If we do not use them in line with God's limits and purposes, they become our masters and we their slaves. They become evil to us, false gods to the true God.

That is why Jesus says we must even hate good things if they hold us back from our life purpose—becoming the people God meant us to be. He tells us that we are to pluck out our eyes or cut off our hands if they offend us or cause us to sin. Likewise, we must be ready to crucify our lesser selves and hate even our family and cherished possessions if they keep us from God and from his purposes for us.

These are not mean commands as we sometimes suppose, but are loving commands. Sacrificing the inferior for something better is like pruning. It produces pain, but that pain is absorbed in the joy we will later feel. The agony of a mother in childbirth may be terrible, but it is nothing in comparison to the happiness that same mother feels when she holds her new child in her arms. As one missionary, who was later killed by the Auca Indians in Ecuador once said, *"He is no fool who gives what he cannot keep to gain what he cannot lose."*

In summary, we love ourselves because God loves us, despite all of our imperfections and foibles. We love ourselves because we believe that God has a purpose and plan for our lives and we want to please him and bring joy to ourselves by aligning our lives with his will. Doing so means pruning that which keeps us from the enjoyment of his presence and cultivating those traits that draw us to him. In this way, we will become the people that God meant us to be.

# CHAPTER 7
## *HOW CAN WE LEARN TO LOVE OURSELVES?*

For the Christian, the basis for loving ourselves in the right way is to love God more than ourselves and to cooperate with him to achieve the plan that he has for our lives. That plan is for us to become a new creature with a new mind, a new heart, and a new will submitted joyfully to God's Will and Truth. We are to become like Jesus, allowing his Spirit to take over our lives and to flow through us like sap from vine to branch.

Becoming like Jesus means that we love others sacrificially as Christ did—ready to give up worldly power, prestige, comfort, wealth, and even our lives if necessary, because of our love for the Father and for each other. Becoming like Jesus means that we would probably restructure our lives and live more simply, retire and pray more often, serve others with the gifts and talents that we have been given, and act with integrity, wisdom, justice, mercy, kindness, courage, confidence, and true humility. Becoming like Jesus, we would not force our beliefs on others, but would leave them with the freedom to choose.

Yet, can we really become good and holy people just like Jesus? Just like Jesus, no. That of course is impossible, because according to Christian doctrine, Jesus was the unique Son of God and one with God and without sin. We, on the other hand, are creatures full of vices and sins.

What then can we practically do to change to become the people that God wants us to be? One option, perhaps, is to wait for God's grace to transform us as we continue to go about our normal activities. Another option, which I feel is more Biblical, is to become a co-worker with God in our own transformation.

# Co-workers with God

Some religions are fatalistic in nature, and those who follow them believe that we can do nothing to change God's plan for each of us. God is the potter and we are the clay. He can make us, break us, mold us, preserve us, or throw us away according to his will. All we can do is submit to his will.

Even some secular persons, who do not believe in a Creator God, have similar fatalistic views. Some believe that we are creatures programmed by our DNA to be what we are. We did not choose our DNA, or where, when, and to whom we were born.

Others believe that our life circumstances determine who we are and what we become. If we were born into poor, abusive families, then we are destined to one type of outcome; and if we were born into wealthy, loving families, our lives will be much different.

Other religions and philosophies of life have a completely different take on things. Their adherents believe that the persons we are and the persons we become is entirely in our own hands. Our fates are not determined by God, but by our own choices and actions. The Hindu and Buddhist believe that we are subject to the law of karma, and our own thoughts, decisions, and actions of past lives and of this life determine our fate in future lives.

Christianity, as I understand it, teaches that the truth is a little of all of the above and more.

Yes, Christianity says, we are creatures of God and God is sovereign with the power to do what he wills with us. Yes, he knows us from before we were born until our final destiny. Yes, we are dependent on God's love and grace for everything, for it is in him that we live, and move, and have our being. Yes, it is also true that we are the products of our DNA and even the product of the decisions made by our ancestors back to Adam and Eve and to their original sin.

41

On the other hand, Christianity also teaches that we are free creatures, whose prayers, decisions, and actions matter. We reap what we sow, and we and our children will benefit or suffer from what we choose and what we do. The bottom line is that we depend on God for everything, including our freedom and salvation, but we are still free creatures responsible for our own destinies. Both statements are true.

We know that we are dependent on God because we did not create ourselves and we cannot sustain our lives without his constant gifts of things like air, water, food, gravity, light, an atmosphere free of deadly chemicals, and so on. The Bible tells us that we cannot add one inch of stature to our height, yet God knows every hair on our head. He also knows when every sparrow falls.

We know that we are free because at every moment of our lives we can choose this or that alternative. Our Deciding Self can opt to listen to one inner voice or another. It can choose to act or not to act.

Christianity therefore teaches our liberty as well as God's sovereignty and his mercy which triumphs over his judgment (James 2:13). It teaches the importance of our own decisions, hard work, and persistence as well as the importance of God's grace in our lives. We love because God first loved us, yet we still must love. He seeks us, but we also must seek, decide, follow, act, and persist. We yearn and believe, but God is the one who gives us that desire for him and that faith. We are drawn to him by his grace and by his love for us, but we are also partners with him in the creation of his kingdom, first in ourselves and then in our world. He is the head, but we are his hands and feet. As Paul says, *"Continue to work out your salvation with fear and trembling for it is God who works in you to will and act according to his good purpose."* (Philippians 2:12-13) He says elsewhere, *"For it is by grace you have been saved, through faith—and this is not from yourselves, it is a gift of God—not by works, so that no one can boast. For we are God's workmanship, created in Christ Jesus to do good works, which God prepared in advance for us to do."* (Ephesians 2:8-10).

The apostle Peter speaks of this working relationship between God and us when he tells us, *"God's power has given us everything we need to lead a godly life. All of that has come to us because we know the One who chose us. He chose us because of his own glory and goodness.*

*He has also given us his very great and valuable promises. He did it so you could share in his nature. He also did it so you could escape from the evil in the world. That evil is caused by sinful longings.*

*So you should try very hard to add goodness to your faith. To goodness, add knowledge. To knowledge, add the ability to control yourselves. To the ability to control yourselves, add the strength to keep going. To the strength to keep going, add godliness. To godliness, add kindness to believers. And to kindness to believers, add love.*

*You should possess more and more of those good points. They will make you useful and fruitful as you get to know our Lord Jesus Christ better."* (2 Peter 1:3-8)

I think that the metaphor of the gardener and garden is very useful for understanding the relationship between God and us, and between grace and works. The gardener by grace is provided with seed, water, soil, sun light, climate, and the miracle of growth. The gardener has little or no control over any of these things in their essence, and he or she can certainly not make a leaf or fruit. Yet the gardener's role is very important too. He or she must believe in the miracle of growth and work hard to bury the seed, pull the weeds, carry the water, scare the birds away, and wait with patience and hope for the results. When the crop is ready, more decisions must be made and work done. The crop needs to be harvested, stored, and then distributed. Choices then need to be made as to the proportions that should be kept for one's own use, that should be used for future seedlings, or that should be sold or given away. The gardener is humble in dependence, grateful for the bounty, and conscious of his or her duties.

Peter says that God draws us to himself and he has given us all that we need to make the journey, but we must turn our face toward him and start walking. Throughout the Bible, we see that God has his role, and we have our role—to train ourselves in godliness; to fight the good fight; to run the race. We are told to use our talents, to lead good and holy lives by loving and being of service to others. We are commanded to think on things that are pure and good, to pray always, to have self-control. We are admonished to tell the truth, to rid ourselves of all malice and deceit, hypocrisy, envy and slander; to heal the sick, to visit those in prison, to take care of the helpless, to encourage others, to give generously, and a host of other things. We are even told to be perfect.

Now we know, of course, that that perfection is impossible without God's grace and intervention. Yet, we also know that we are called to do our part to become the good and useful persons that we were meant to be. How do we do that? Here are a few suggestions that I find useful for myself.

## TRAINING OURSELVES TO BE AND DO GOOD

**Become aware:** *Know yourself!* So often, we look, but we do not really see; we hear, but we really do not understand. Awareness is a fundamental prerequisite for understanding, empathy, and holiness. It is the foundation of wisdom, worship, and charitable action. Jesus said, *"He who has ears, let him hear."* (Matthew 11:15) So often, we do not take time to listen or to see as we should.

With awareness, we look inside and see our many selves, our failures and sin, as well as our potential for good. Saint Paul shares his view of what he saw when he looked within himself:

*"I do not understand what I do. For what I want to do I do not do, but what I hate I do. And if I do what I do not want to do, I agree that the law is good. As it is, it is no longer I myself who do it, but it is sin living in me. I know that nothing good lives in me, that is, in my sinful nature. For I have the desire to do what is good, but I cannot carry it out. For what I do is not the good I want to do; no, the evil I do not want to do, this I keep on doing. Now if I do what I do not want to do, it is no longer I who do it, but it is sin living in me that does it. So I find this law at work: When I want to do good, evil is right there with me. For in my inner being I delight in God's law; but I see another law at work in the members of my body,*

*waging war against the law of my mind and making me a prisoner of the law of sin at work within my members. What a wretched man I am! Who will rescue me from this body of death? Thanks be to God, through Jesus Christ our Lord!* (Romans 7:15-25)

Awareness reveals not only our many conflicting selves, but also the Spirit of God within us. Only with awareness can we hear the still, small voice of God and distinguish it from all of our clamoring selves and the spirits of darkness. With awareness, we not only see ourselves as we really are, we also get a glimpse of what we could become.

With awareness, we understand that certain paths lead to unhappiness and destruction even though they might look smooth and inviting at the outset. On the other hand, we also understand that paths that look painful and impossible to follow at first can lead to happiness and fulfillment. Awareness gives us wisdom and balance.

With awareness, we also begin to see others—really see them. We empathize with them; we feel their sorrow and rejoice with them in their happiness. We understand better why they are who they are and we see the potential of who they can become. They become friends instead of objects that we manipulate and use for our own purposes.

With awareness, we realize that the surest road to self-perfection is to love something greater than we are. When we love something more important than we are, we forget our lower selves in the vision of the higher, and we become happier people. Some people find delight in a hobby, project, or meditation in which they can forget themselves for a short time. Others find delight in pleasing others. Loving God with all of our heart, however, is the surest way to self-transformation because we will want to become like the beloved, the highest, the best, and the purest that we can imagine.

**Yearn:** Buddhists speak of getting rid of desire as a necessary step for liberation. Christians, Jews, and Muslims do not go that far. They see that desires are like motors, and when they are good, they can lead us to God, and when they are evil, they can lead us away from him.

In our reading of the lives of saints, we notice their passion for God. The language that they use is often like that of a lover yearning for his or her beloved. One also sees the intense pain they feel at the sufferings of the world and at their own failings. Paul, considered as one of the greatest saints of Christianity, thought himself as one of the worst sinners.

The saints have this passion for God because they are truly aware of how good and holy God really is and of how unhappy and unholy they are without him. They yearn for excellence, for that which changes not. They have been able *"to taste and see that the Lord is good."* (Psalm 34:8) They trust fully the truth of what Paul says that *"no eye has seen nor ear heard, nor has it entered into the mind of man what God has prepared for them who love him."* (1 Corinthians 2:9) They believe firmly that *"You will fill me with joy in your presence"* (Psalm 16:11), and they yearn for that presence and that joy.

**Decide:** It is very difficult to generate that kind of yearning if we do not already have it. Either we have a passion for God and his Goodness and repugnance for evil or we do not. If we do not have it, then we can at least <u>will</u> to have such a desire. Our Deciding Self can start by admitting our failures and imperfections as a clear reality and then pray for both a yearning for the good and disgust for the evil that we see within and without us.

Since God commands us to love, then it must mean that love is tied more to our will and our Deciding Self than to our emotional selves. Our Deciding Self can choose and act on commands, while our emotional selves cannot always. We therefore must love ourselves by the decisions that we make.

We make decisions all day long. Some are very large ones about life goals, vocations, character changes, and beliefs; some are smaller ones such as how to use our time, what to eat or drink, what to say, how to spend our money, what to do, and even what to concentrate on in our minds at any given moment. These decisions, small and large, beginning in childhood and ending in death, have an important impact on our actions and therefore on our habits, character, and destiny. That is why we should be very mindful of each decision's importance.

Our highest goal should be to merge the will of our Deciding Self with the Will of the Holy Spirit within us so that all of our daily decisions are in tune with Ultimate Reality, the way things are and should be. When that happens we can say with Paul, *"I have been crucified with Christ and I no longer live, but Christ lives in me."* (Galatians 2:20)

**Act:** As we noted previously, we really do not make a decision until we act on it. Acting reinforces the decision and makes it clear to ourselves and to others where we stand.

Sometimes our acts cause us only pleasure, and sometime they cause us only pain. Most of the time, however, they cause us <u>both</u> pleasure and pain.

For example, an act of charity might cause us suffering in our Dark and Skeptical selves because we have to give up our time, our freedom, our goods, our lusts, our pride, and our comfort in order to perform the act. However, that same act of charity can also create a deep joy in our Yearning and Deciding selves because we know that we are doing the right thing and serving God and others.

In the same way, an act of selfishness and sin can cause immediate pleasure in the Dark and Skeptical selves, but cause pain and suffering in the Yearning and Deciding selves. It is a paradox, but happiness and suffering can exist side by side in the same act.

Wise persons are aware of this and therefore they strive to do what is both right and good. They know that the joys of the Yearning and Deciding selves are deeper and longer lasting than the pleasures of the Dark and Skeptical selves. They also know that if they make a habit of doing good out of a response to the leadings of the Yearning self or Holy Spirit, doing good will eventually become easier and even more pleasurable. They know that if they apply the little light and understanding that they have, more light will be given to them. If they are faithful stewards with the few talents that they have, then more will be given to them. If on the other hand, they are not faithful and do not act, then even the little that they have may be taken away from them. We have to act.

We know that we will always have pain and suffering in our lives. If we concentrate our attention on that pain and do not see beyond it, then we will increase its power over us. However, if we look beyond the immediate pain to some joyful hope, like a hiker facing storms, cold, and exhaustion striving for the peak, then the pain becomes much less intense. Senseless pain, which is terrible to endure, becomes pain with meaning and purpose, and therefore, much easier to bear.

With this awareness, what are some specific ways we can act to better prepare us to be more loving and more useful to God in creating a better world? Here are a few suggestions:

***Act by changing our attitudes with study, meditation, and prayer:*** We can work at changing our attitudes by putting aside time for study and meditation on the fatherhood of God, on his love for us, and on his holiness and rejection of evil. Studying the Bible and other spiritual writings is something that we can do to feed our minds and souls. We can meditate on God's purpose for us, for the world, and on how we can best act to bring in his kingdom. We can meditate on the life and teachings of Christ and on those of his followers. We can meditate on the lives of other good men within and without our religion and on how God uses them. We can meditate on the impermanence of life, of wealth, of lust, and of worldly beauty, and on the certainty of death. We can ponder how evil leads ultimately to chaos and despair despite momentary gratification, while goodness brings ultimate happiness, contentment, and peace. We can meditate on the virtues and their importance. We can think of how they make life beautiful and how vices lead to unhappiness. As the Bible teaches, we can take our thoughts captive and think about whatever is true, whatever is noble, whatever is right, whatever is pure, whatever is lovely, whatever is admirable, excellent, or praiseworthy. (Philippians 4:8)

One caution: When we meditate on our failings, it is important not to strengthen them by paying too much attention to them. If we sit and meditate only on our failures and not on the goodness of God and the needs of others, then we become self-centered, self-despairing, or self-righteous. We need balance.

During my graduate studies, I worked in a well-known university hospital as a psychiatric aide. For the greater part of the day, as part of their treatment, the bright young patients thought about and talked about themselves constantly—to their doctors, to the nurses and aides, to social workers and to each other. While certainly self-awareness is important, I always wondered if such total concentration on oneself was the way to health or was it instead a reinforcement of their sickness. Would it not be more productive and conducive to true happiness if we could get out of ourselves or submerge ourselves in a bigger life and purpose?

Meditation and prayer help us to do just that. They help us to become absorbed in God's life, purpose, and will and not in our own. They help us become new creatures, as thoughts of God's goodness and love begin to permeate our minds and then our lives. They are the basis of our part in self-transformation.

***Act by consciously thinking of others:*** By meditating on God, we begin to see him in all creation. We start to understand others in the light of his love and purposes for them. We empathize with them in their struggles and pleasures and see them as brothers and sisters, children like us of the same Father, parts of the same body. We begin to wish their good just as we wish our own, and thus slowly lose our prejudices and hardness of heart. We say silent prayers for their well-being as we come to understand that life is a team sport and that we are all in this together. Their progress and virtues will add to our happiness just as ours will theirs.

***Act by imitating Christ:*** We can practice being the person we want to be, but are not yet. Like a budding painter, musician, or mathematician, we have to learn from our teacher and practice the basics of our craft constantly. Over time, talents that are so difficult at first, become natural and easier. Finally, our grasp of the material becomes so great that it becomes a part of our being. We do not just paint pictures, play music, or do math; we become painters, musicians, and mathematicians. The same is true with the virtues. They, too, will become a part of our being. Our goal is not just to refrain from telling a lie; it is to become honest persons whose very gut wrenches at any falsehood. It is not just to do kind acts; it is to become loving, compassionate people like Christ. It is not just to do good deeds; it is to become good and virtuous persons.

More than likely, we will find that our motivations for good actions are very mixed at first and therefore impure. One part of us really wants to be and do good for God's sake and because we know that this is the way that we should live. Another part of us, however, wants to do good for whatever we can get out of it. We want to impress, manipulate, win merit or praise, or win position and power by our words or actions.

What do we do? We do not want to be hypocrites who pretend to be good in order to get things for ourselves. If we do that, we are like the Pharisees, the very people most condemned by Jesus. Yet, we do want to train ourselves in godliness, to become what we are not yet, to become more Christ-like.

There is a difference in a hypocrite, a saint, and a person hoping to be a saint, even though they all may do the same good deed.

The hypocrite does the good deed mainly to fool and manipulate others for his or her own purposes. The hypocrite's primary motivation is selfish, to get some benefit out of a situation for himself or herself and not so much to benefit the other.

The saint does the good deed out of love for God and for the other. The saint's main motivation is for the other's good.

We, who want to be saints, do the good deed out of mixed emotions. We recognize our selfish motivations and are honest about them, as we do not want to fool anyone and be hypocrites. Yet, we also want to do the good, not so much because we yet care greatly about the other person, but because we want to care about the other. We do not yet love God with all of our heart and our neighbor as ourselves, but we <u>want</u> to one day be capable of that type of love.

If God has not yet transformed our hearts, then the only road that we know to take is to train ourselves with God's help. We "act as if" we were good people, even though we are not yet. We do the good deed or the caring and right thing even though our inner emotions are not pure. We decide to act generously even though we know that we are not feeling generous inside. We act courageously even though we are full of fear. We act with kindness even though we care little for the other.

This pretension is not hypocrisy if behind it all is the yearning for goodness and not the desire to manipulate. It is training in godliness. It is putting on a mask in the hope that the mask will one day mold the face behind it to become like it. It is the child imitating the way his father does something in the desire to one day be like the father. It is not yet true, but the hope is that one day it will be. As we act on the little flicker of desires for the good, we hope that God will increase those desires in our heart and our competence in our actions.

***Act by holding ourselves accountable:*** We have to constantly review our progress and hold ourselves accountable to God, ourselves, and to people whose love we feel and whose wisdom we trust. We do not always see ourselves as others see us. Some of their impressions may be false, but others hit the mark much better than our own wishful visions of ourselves. Criticism hurts, but the wise person will learn to use it to identify blemishes in himself or herself that need eradicating. Constructive criticism by others is a useful gift and a reality check even though our natural tendency is to resist it as it hurts. The key to humility is to see criticism not as a debasement of our selves, but as realistic and helpful pruning.

***Act by picking ourselves up with humor and determination:*** Humor is a great gift from God. When it is self-deprecating humor, it reveals a trust that other persons will recognize their own foibles and mistakes in our own, that they will therefore not condemn us, but will empathize with us in laughter and mutual embarrassment. Failure is certain as we progress towards the Good, but so is God's love for us despite our failures. The certainty of God's love helps us to renew our determination to do better the next time. We can learn valuable lessons from our failures, trusting God for forgiveness. Because of his forgiveness, we can even learn to forgive ourselves.

***Act by developing skills:*** One of the definitions of good is that it is something that fulfills its purpose and is useful. "Loving ourselves" therefore means not only learning to be good inside by imitating Christ and practicing the virtues, but also learning skills that will make us useful to God, ourselves, and to others.

Despite our many similarities, people are also very different from each other. We are born in different cultures and in different economic and political systems. We are also born with differing innate emotional tendencies and differing physical and intellectual possibilities. Some of us have inborn potential and desire to become musicians and others to be farmers; some to be counselors and others to be engineers. Whatever our natural level of potential or desire, we want to be as good as we can at what we choose to do.

All vocations that help others should be valued. Society needs us all to make our communities function well, just as the hand needs the eye and the ear needs the mouth. The loss of one part has a profound effect on all of the others. Therefore, it behooves us to choose and value our professions in terms of their usefulness to others instead of merely in terms of their prestige and the money associated with them. Likewise, we should value the vocations of others because of their usefulness to us. An irony of life is that some of the highest paying professions are the least useful to us, while some of the lowest paying, are the most useful.

*Life skills:* In preparing ourselves to be useful, we need to learn so many life skills. As a baby and toddler, we learn to control our bodies; we learn how to interpret the things around us and to communicate in a myriad of different languages. As we grow older, we learn to identify, dissect, and solve problems. We learn how to find, organize, and use information and how to communicate well to others verbally and in writing. Other life skills we learn are how to listen, to think, to evaluate arguments, and to come to our own decisions. We also learn virtues like honesty, dependability, and persistence, and social graces that help reduce friction and competition in our relations with others.

*Semi-professional skills:* There are also many practical skills to learn. These facilitate our daily lives as well as those of our families, friends, and work associates. These are skills like cooking, plumbing, electricity, carpentry, mechanics, driving, gardening, animal care, typing, and the use of computers. They are skills like basic planning, budgeting, investing, researching, language learning, and teaching.

*Professional skills:* Finally, we need to learn the deeper skills that are important to the vocations that we have chosen for ourselves. To be proficient in some professions requires years of study and constant upgrading in order to be effective as knowledge advances and new situations occur. Whatever the profession we choose, we should try to be the best that we can in it so that we can be useful to others. That should be our main goal.

In summary, loving ourselves in the right way means many things. Most of all, it means training and transforming ourselves under God's direction, power, and grace into the sons and daughters of God that we were meant to be. It means being conscious of our sin and of his love for us despite that sin. It means wanting more and more to do his will and more and more to offer ourselves to be channels of his love to those around us and to the rest of his creation. It means by his grace, developing skills and character so that we can serve others the best that we can.

# CHAPTER 8
## *WHAT DOES IT MEAN TO LOVE OUR NEIGHBOR AS OURSELVES?*

In earlier chapters, we have argued how God's love for us and our love for God, are the Christian's basis for being and doing good. We have also discussed how loving ourselves in the proper way brings us happiness and helps us prepare ourselves to love and do good to others. Now let us turn our attention to the third part of Jesus' map to goodness—learning to love our neighbor as ourselves.

Loving our neighbor <u>as</u> ourselves is what doing good means to most of us. I have underlined the word "as" because it is in that little word that much of the difficulty lies. It is not hard for us to love others a little because we know that we need each other. However, to love them as much as we love ourselves seems impossible for many of us. Loving in that way goes against our basic instincts, and we have to be pulled "kicking and screaming" into giving up our time, our comfort, our wealth, and our honor to others.

Earlier, we considered the anxiety many of us feel as we are daily confronted with situations in which our own desires and needs conflict with those of others. This anxiety is partially because we do not have clear answers to questions like the following: *What is the good that we should do to others? Why should we do good anyway? Whom should we help? How should we help?*

If we can find personally satisfying answers to these questions, maybe then we will be able to make better decisions about helping others and find the peace that eludes us. Therefore, let us look briefly at these questions one by one.

# WHAT IS THE GOOD THAT WE SHOULD DO TO OTHERS?

If loving others means to will and work for their good, then a host of new questions come to us as we try to decide how to act. First, how do we determine what is good for someone else when we are hardly even sure what is good for ourselves? Is it what we consider good for them? Is it what they would consider good for themselves? Is it what others want for them? Or, is it what God wants for them? If it is the latter, how do we determine what God wants?

Adding to these difficulties, we have seen that what we consider good has a tendency to change from person to person and moment to moment. What is good for one person may turn out to be terrible for another. What is good in the short run may end up being very bad in the long run. What is good for the flesh may not be good for the spirit. How do we therefore come up with good decisions and good actions?

People are different and have different wants and needs according to their sex, their age, their abilities, their culture, their economic and social position, their DNA, and their beliefs. What I want for myself may not be what you want for yourself. I love solitude and quiet, while another might love socializing and loud music. A child wants to receive everything she desires in a store, but her parents know that if they cave in and fulfill her desires, they will eventually end up paupers and run the risk of turning their child into a spoiled tyrant.

Another problem is that there is little consistency in our own concepts of good and bad. One moment, I silently curse the selfish people who will not let me into a faster traffic lane. The next moment, I become that selfish person, and curse the person who is trying to butt into my lane in front of me! Therefore, if our own definitions of what is good are so variable and unstable, how in the world can we come up with a method for determining what is good for others?

There is, of course, no infallible method for determining the good that we should do in every single situation. There are instead general rules that help orient our actions like "Do unto others as you would have them do unto you," "Love and do as you please," or "Win-win." However, they often create many more questions as we enter into the details of a situation.

Moral rules of behavior such as "You should not steal" or "You should always tell the truth" are like rules of grammar, applicable in most cases. Yet, like rules of grammar, they usually have exceptions. For example, some would argue that to protect the life of someone it may be necessary to lie—to tell the murderer seeking his prey that his victim went in the opposite direction. Similarly, it may be acceptable to steal in order to get food for your children to live. In these cases, the greater good trumps the evil or the lesser good.

These moral rules of behavior and their exceptions are remarkably universal and reinforced by scriptures, philosophy, psychology, and by common sense and experience. The main tenet of our moral grammar is the notion that human beings have worth and dignity, just because of the fact that we exist. The Bible and experience teach us that we are higher creatures than animals, plants, and minerals. While we should care for our environment for selfish and unselfish reasons, our needs as humans take final precedence over those of rocks, plants, and even animals. Human life and happiness should be protected and promoted before all else.

In order for us to continue to exist and to be happy as humans, we need to meet certain conditions. We already know most of them, but it is useful to remind ourselves of their importance. The psychologist Abraham Maslov ranks these conditions in a well-known pyramid with the observation that when one level of our needs is met, then we re-focus our attention on the next higher level. While many disagree about the number and types of different levels that he describes, still, this is an insight that helps explain to us why people have different ideas as to what is best for them at different times.

At the base of the pyramid, Maslov puts our physiological needs for air, food, water, and sleep. If we are deprived of them, then nothing is more important to our good and happiness than to get them. Therefore, one aspect of the good that we should do for others is to make sure that people have these basic resources for survival. We are to feed the hungry, to give water to those who are thirsty, to clothe the naked, and to give rest to the weary.

The second layer of Maslov's pyramid is our need for safety. Once we have satisfied our basic needs for air, food, water, and sleep, we turn our attention to wanting to protect our supply of them and thus our well-being. Therefore, a second type of good we can do for others is to ensure their safety. We can do this by modifying our own behavior and by promoting and enforcing rules in our communities that concern the safety of others. Safety, in the sense we are using it, means not only personal safety from assault and harm, but safety from extreme want. It means predictability in our relationships and, as much as possible, protection from accidents, theft, and other dangers. The Bible pays special attention to our duties to protect the rights and safety of the weaker ones of our communities such as children, strangers, widows, orphans, the sick, and the disabled.

The third level in Maslov's pyramid is the level of love and belonging. We all want to belong and to be valued since we are social creatures. "No man is an island unto himself." We seek out spouses, and then hope for children in order to form our families. We align ourselves with friends and social groups of people who are like-minded with us. We join clubs, religious organizations, and movements. Therefore, another aspect of the good that we should do for others is to promote the rights of people to freely marry, form families, raise their children, associate with people of like-mind, and promote their causes. The Bible teaches us that we are to come together and to share; to rejoice with those who rejoice and to mourn with those who mourn. We are to comfort, encourage, and care for our brothers and sisters in the world.

The fourth level of our needs, according to Maslov, is for status and esteem. We do not just want to join groups, we want to be considered useful and respected members of those groups. We want to have important roles and positions and to be acclaimed and remembered for our abilities and contributions.

At this point, doing good becomes a little more complicated. It is somewhat straightforward to provide for the physical needs of populations of people, for their safety, and even for their freedom to form families and to freely associate in groups. It is much more difficult to insure that their needs for status and esteem are met. Not all of us can be president of the organization, or the best athlete on the team, or the smartest person in the class. However, we can do good by encouraging, praising, and thanking people where we can. We can also remind them of their great and eternal value as children loved by God the Father.

Perhaps the best way to help others fulfill their need for status and esteem is to encourage them to change their attitude as to what status is. Jesus did that when two of his disciples came to him with their mother requesting high-ranking positions for themselves in his coming kingdom. Jesus turned the prestige game on its head by telling them that those who want to be great in the kingdom should seek instead to be the least, the servant of all. He did this same sort of contrary thinking in the Beatitudes with our ideas of happiness. If we could turn our desires from wanting to be served into wanting to serve, we would all be truly happy.

Finally, Maslov puts our need for self-actualization as our highest and most refined need. We want to be the best we can be and fulfill our potentials. This need causes me to write this book and you to read it. We want to be the people we were meant to be, to live the best lives that we possibly can, and to help others realize their potentials. The greatest good Christians believe that they can do for others is to help them come into a loving relationship with God the Father. That is because Christians believe that it is in this relationship that ultimate happiness and fulfillment reside.

Maslov's pyramid, of course, is only one of the many guides that furnish us with practical ideas about the good we should do to others. The United Nations' "Declaration of the Universal Rights of Man" and "Millennium Development Goals" are two others. The "Declaration of the Universal Rights of Man" emphasizes the dignity and worth of all individuals. It promotes the good of people around the world through goals that emphasize social progress and better standards of living. It underlines one's right to be free, safe, and treated justly as well as one's right to work, to leisure, to adequate food, clothing, housing, medical care, social services, and to support in the time of unemployment, sickness, or disability. The Declaration also promotes the right to education as it is through education that we learn the skills to support ourselves and to be useful. It underlines the importance of freedom, of understanding, of tolerance, and of the respect of other nations, racial and religious groups. Such respect is fundamental to world peace and prosperity.

The United Nation's "Millennium Development Goals" stipulates eight measurable targets for the world to meet in order to promote the welfare of all. They are to eradicate extreme poverty and hunger; achieve universal primary education; promote gender equality and empower women; reduce child mortality; improve maternal health; combat HIV/AIDS, malaria and other diseases; ensure environmental sustainability; and develop a global partnership for development. All of these things are part of the good that we should strive for as individuals and as nations.

Thus in summary, the good that we should do to others is multifaceted—physical, psychological, and spiritual. As humans, we are body, soul, and spirit, and our happiness depends on meeting the needs of each individual in each of these areas.

## *WHY SHOULD WE DO GOOD?*

There are many reasons for doing good, some more selfish than others. Sometimes we do good primarily for our own gain. We want to escape punishment or to win something positive in return—eternal life, money, power, praise, an engraved plaque, or just a good warm sense of happiness that we are doing the right thing. We may enjoy helping others and problem solving. We gain dignity from having something worthwhile to give. We are pleased when people thank us and others praise us. We take pleasure in the camaraderie of our fellow workers. When we do good, we feel a little relief from the guilt and pain of knowing that we have so much and others have so little; we feel relief from the condemnation of God and of others for not living the life that we are supposed to live.

Sometimes we do good because it is our <u>duty</u> to do good. Doing good is the way we feel that we should live and that others should live. Sometimes what motivates us is a religious or social duty; other times it is professional duty. As salaried employees in social work, medicine, economic development, ministry, and so many other professions, it is our job to do good. We may have no real emotional concern for the person we are helping, but at least we would like to have such a concern. Doing good may be a "will" thing to us rather than a "feeling" one.

Sometimes we do good because we have real <u>empathy</u> for the persons we are helping. In this case, our concentration is not so much on our own needs, but on the needs of the person we are trying to help. Rewards for doing good may come, but these are not our main reason for acting. We do good because we care, and therefore it is a natural thing to do.

While empathy for others and a sincere desire to see their good should be the motivation that we aim for, it is difficult to eliminate our own material and emotional needs from the equation. Every good action that we do is selfish in some way. Purifying our motivations means recognizing them for what they are, both selfish and unselfish. It means being truthful about them to ourselves and to others and to pray to God to turn them into a sincere desire to serve and to help.

## WHOM SHOULD WE HELP?

Jesus tells us to do good to all persons and to give to whoever asks. At first, that seems like an impossible task, as we have limited time and resources. Helping one person may mean that we do not have enough resources to help another. Positions of authority and honor are also limited. As we have already noted, placing someone in a position means that another applicant is denied the job.

While we should try to do good to all, (even to our enemies according to Jesus' teaching), we need to establish a certain order in how we go about doing that good. For example, the Bible tells us that God wants all people to be saved. Yet, Jesus followed a set program for bringing this about. First, he chose twelve disciples and taught them. Then he and his disciples took their message mainly to the children of Israel. Only after his resurrection did he send his followers into all nations. Likewise, Jesus only cured those people who came to him and who believed, and not all of the sick and disabled of the world.

We too have to prioritize whom to help, so let us look now at some of the factors that determine our priorities:

*Our awareness level:* We help those people whose needs we see, who come into our lives in some way or another. Someone stumbles by our side, and we reach out and pick them up. Someone asks us for money and we give it. A newspaper article or television program highlights a person or condition that tugs at our emotions, and we want to help, even if it is someone on the other side of the globe.

The needs of our family, school, church, workplace, and neighborhood are usually high priority for us because they are constantly on our radar. Other people and causes, even if they might be more deserving, do not get our help because we do not know about them. Because awareness is a pre-requisite for giving, philanthropic organizations try to keep the needs of their causes in front of us at all times with news articles, advertisements, events, and constant appeals through calls and mailings. Today, because of the internet and satellite TV, so many worthy needs and causes come into our consciousness every day that we often feel overwhelmed by them.

*The perceived importance of the need:* We all have needs. When we try to determine whom we should help, we quickly calculate how important the need of that person is. We ask ourselves what will be the immediate and long-term effect on that person if we help or do not help. Is their need urgent? (For example, someone is drowning, and we are the only one close by to help.) Is their need something less urgent? (For example, a beggar on a busy street corner asks us for food money.) In this latter case, we may be hesitant to give because we do not see any urgency or importance. Many others besides us can help. Anyway, we imagine that the beggar is going to use the money for alcohol or drugs and not for food.

*Our assessment of our own resources:* We have to do a kind of mental triage. Do we have the immediate means or skills that are needed in the specific incident? Will our lack of skills or physical ability actually end up harming the person we want to help? Are we able to swim or do we have a life buoy to throw to the drowning person? Do we understand basic medical procedures enough and the dangers of their misuse? Do we have the money or time to help?

*Our level of responsibility to the person being helped:* Most of us feel that we have a hierarchy of responsibilities to people. First, we are responsible to those for whom we have natural lifetime commitments, such as to our families and to our "tribes." Second, we are responsible to those to whom we have made commitments, like to our employer, our church, our nation, and other groups we have joined. Third, we are responsible to those whom God places in our daily paths and who are therefore our neighbors. Finally, we are responsible to anyone else that God leads us to care for, especially the supposed "losers" of society—the rejected like prostitutes, prisoners, the poor, the sick, the disabled, the ugly, and the problematic.

Consciously and subconsciously, we consider all of these things and other questions like *how will helping this person or organization benefit them? How will helping them affect us in loss of time, money, comfort? How will helping them benefit us in terms of our feeling good about ourselves, of others being pleased with us, and of God being pleased with us? How will helping them affect our ability to help others for whom we are also responsible? How will not helping them affect us?* Not helping has potential costs too. There can be legal costs (if we are criminally negligent); material costs (others in the future may decide not to help us if we refuse to help them); and psychological costs (such as feelings of shame and guilt).

# *HOW SHOULD WE HELP?*

There are many ways to do good to others. We can be prophetic and warn them of possible moral, physical, or social danger. We can teach and offer encouragement. We can support others with our votes, our labor, or tools. We can give money or goods. We can do good now and after our deaths, through the legacies we leave, the institutions we have founded, and the teachings and examples we have imparted. We can do good individually, or we can work with others in informal coalitions or in formal organizations. We will examine more specific ways of doing good in another part of this book, but our marching orders are always to do good. As John Wesley said, "Do all the good you can, by all the means you can, in all the places you can, at all the times you can, to all the people you can, as long as ever you can."

Perhaps the basic principle we should follow in doing good is to <u>do no harm.</u> Well-intended actions often have unexpected negative consequences. Collateral damage always seems to be a possibility, in war and in normal life. Parents are especially aware of these unexpected dangers. If children are overly protected from germs, falls, and failures, they cannot build up the necessary resistance and knowledge to confront similar problems as adults. If children get all they want early in life, they might not learn how to deal with scarcity and difficulties in the future.

People involved in economic development projects are also very aware of this maxim. So often, well-intentioned do-gooders may resolve an immediate problem, but in the process of helping, they end up causing much more complicated troubles. For example, when a country receives free or heavily subsidized food for a long time, local farmers may decide not to plant and harvest because their meager profits are not worth the hard work involved. When minority groups are given special considerations in entry exams for universities and then in grades and exit exams, their credentials become suspect to employers and their own sense of self-esteem is undermined. Likewise, when institutions take care of all of the needs of persons for many years, these person can become psychologically dependent and unwilling to leave even if they are capable of surviving on their own on the outside. We need great wisdom to "do no harm."

A second way of doing good is <u>to actively prevent the bad from happening.</u> We do this by our prophetic warnings, or by establishing laws that regulate what individuals and institutions can do and cannot do in a society. These laws prohibit actions like the harming of our environment and the threatening the life, liberty, and property of others. They protect the weak and vulnerable like young children, the sick, the pregnant, the old, the disabled, and racial and religious minorities. Doing good is a balancing act between allowing as much individual freedom as we can and protecting others from that freedom.

Of course, the third main way of doing good is <u>to be proactive.</u> Good is not just the absence of evil, it is a positive thing. Doing good is not only preventing or reacting to bad situations, but it involves fostering growth, beauty, and happiness. We can bring joy and fulfillment to people through acts of kindness, through creations of art, and through wise counsel. Kindness is the salt of life and beauty is the pepper.

As we seek to do good to others, we should always try our best to be *relevant*—to deal with real problems and not just do good to make ourselves feel virtuous. We should try to be *effective*—to find solutions that actually work; to be *efficient*—to use limited resources in the best possible manner so that there is a surplus to solve other pressing problems; and to be *fair*—so that in solving a problem for one person or segment of society, we do not ignore the problems of others. Our solutions should also be as *sustainable* as possible—to help people become less dependent on us so that they can provide for their own needs and even join the ranks of those whose surplus allows them to help others. As Jesus said in his teachings, our greatest happiness is not in receiving, but in giving. It is not in being served, but in serving.

Self-sufficiency is a key goal for any long-term, successful program for doing good. We do good to our children by protecting them when they are vulnerable, but also by giving them the will and the skills to eventually move out from the home to be on their own and become giving parents and members of society themselves. Likewise, we do good in our societal programs, not only by offering relief to people when they are vulnerable, but also by helping them become self-sufficient so that they can not only take care of themselves, but also of others.

One reason that self-sufficiency is such an important goal is efficiency. If a person, program, or society becomes self-sufficient and sustainable, then that frees up limited time and resources to address other needy causes. If a person or program becomes profitable, then new resources are created for helping others. The former recipient of assistance may now become a donor of aid. One of the greatest joys I had from my work with disabled persons in Brazil was seeing those trained and placed in jobs becoming financial contributors to the organization that helped them.

Another reason to promote self-sufficiency is example. Success breeds success. People, who are down-and-out, are encouraged when they see that others, who were once like themselves, have overcome their problems. They can learn from them the successful strategies that helped them turn around their lives. The best mentor to an alcoholic is an ex-alcoholic.

Finally, self-sufficiency gives us a sense of dignity. We feel better about ourselves if we have something of value to contribute to others. So often, when people describe why they became involved in community service, they say that they wanted to give back something to society. A paradoxical but true spiritual law of happiness is that in doing good to others, one does good to oneself, and in giving happiness, one also receives happiness. Therefore, in teaching others to give, we are showing them a better way for them to be happy.

# CHAPTER 9

## HOW CAN WE LEARN TO LOVE OUR NEIGHBOR AS OURSELVES?

The task of loving others <u>as</u> ourselves seems to me to be quite impossible without God's grace and his transforming power in our lives and in our world. To love others as ourselves, we need the power of God flowing through us. We know that we cannot do it on our own, but even so, Jesus commands us to act.

In previous chapters, we have discussed many steps that we can take to help us learn to love God and to love ourselves in the right way. All of these actions are also useful for helping us to love our neighbor. Added to these, I would like to mention a few others.

First, we can continually <u>try to join our hearts and wills with God's so that he can use us as channels</u> for his light, wisdom, love, and healing power to others. We need to search for the signals of his will and then connect with them and let them permeate us and flow through us to others.

For many years, we went without internet access on our farm in Brazil because we were in the middle of a large pine forest whose trees blocked the waves that came from the cell towers many kilometers away. We found, though, after much experimenting, that the signals that did not reach our house, came through strongly in different areas of the pasture. So now, when we want to go on the internet, we take our fold-up chairs and laptops and sit among the cows, the hogs, and the geese, connecting to the signals that in turn connect us to our friends around the world. This action of putting ourselves in the path of internet signals from the tower is a metaphor for how we can act to put ourselves in the path of God's signals by actively opening ourselves to him and listening to him in prayer and meditation and scripture reading.

Through this seeking and listening, we form a vision in our minds of God's purpose for us, for those closest to us, and for our world. From what we gather from scripture and from our own inner yearnings, God's desire is for all of us to become his sons and daughters, united to him and to each other in *agape* or sacrificial love. He created the world and called it good, so his desire is a world of good—of beauty and not of ugliness; of growth rather than decay. It is a world of kindness and sharing rather than of egotism; of peace rather than of war; of plenty rather than of scarcity. His desire is a world of truth rather than of lies; of humility rather than of pride; of justice and mercy rather than of injustice and revenge; of life rather than of death; of hope rather than of despair; of laughter rather than of gloom; of unity rather than of disunity; and of trust rather than of distrustful anxiety. It is a world where all is in submission to God's Goodness, Truth, and Love—the Ultimate Reality of the universe. Our roles on this earth are to work for this type of world both in ourselves and in others—competing with each other in doing good deeds for one another.

A third step we can take is to compare ourselves and our world to that vision. Obviously, the reality is that we are far from that ideal. The world and the people around us are full of defects just as are we, but the good news is that we also have tremendous potential because we are made in God's image and are beloved by him. We are a mixture of egotism and idealism, of virtues and faults, of skills and needs, of knowledge and ignorance. We have fears and limitations, but also strengths and talents.

We should try our best, with God's grace, to develop the good, not only within us, but also in our neighbor, and in the rest of God's creation. We are our brothers' keeper and they are ours. We need each other. Empathetic awareness of other creatures, both human and non-human, of their services to us and of their needs is a pre-requisite for loving them and for doing them good. The more we become aware of them, the more we understand, empathize, and are grateful for them. The more we understand, empathize, and are grateful for them, the more we love and want to do good to them. The more we love and do good to them, the more we bring in God's kingdom.

A fourth step is to <u>develop a personal strategy</u> for cooperating with God to transform ourselves and the rest of creation from that which we are into that which we were meant to be. That is what this little book is for me—my personal strategy. I hope it will also be useful to you as well and help you to develop your own strategy. With the help of mentors, scripture, and the Holy Spirit, we need to think through who we really are and what is our individual vocation and purpose in this short life. God has created each of us with special talents and with differing spheres of influence. What should be our special role in bringing in his kingdom and how should we prepare for that role? What should be our short and long-term strategies for the sanctification of ourselves and of our world? How can we cooperate with God and with his other servants to bring in his kingdom? How can we best fit in and have a positive impact in our ever-widening circles of family, community, nation, and world?

Fifth, we need to <u>apply our strategies</u> on a daily basis. Jesus calls for doers of his word and not just hearers and planners. We are told that those who truly love him will actually act on his instructions—to share the good news, to heal the sick, to feed the hungry, to clothe the naked, to comfort the grieving, to rejoice with those who rejoice, to welcome the stranger, to visit those who are in prison, and to give to those in need. We can do this as individuals and as partners with others working through organizations.

Sixth, we should <u>constantly evaluate our actions and our progress</u>. At the end of the day, it is useful to sit down and quietly evaluate how successful we have been in carrying out our personal strategies. Where did we succeed or fail? Were our motives what they should have been? What kind of difference did we really make in the lives of others? During the day, were we able to be loving, kind, truthful, and wise, or were we mostly selfish? How do we think that God, or those whom we tried to help that day, would evaluate our efforts? How can we improve in our thoughts and actions?

Seventh, we need to <u>ask forgiveness</u> for where we have failed in thought, word, and deed and to <u>give thanks to God</u> for where we have succeeded. Our little attempts to change ourselves, to love others, and to change our world for the better are always full of failures. Every day, we are probably amazed and discouraged at how little progress we make. I know I am! Most days, I do not even try to follow my own advice!

Yet, we are confident that God, more than anyone, knows our inner weakness. We trust in his forgiveness, and that in his goodness, mercy, and power, he will use our weak efforts for his purposes. All things, even our failures, serve him, especially if we have set our heart and will on following him as best we can.

In summary, therefore, we learn to love others because we believe that God our Father first loved us and that he wills that we love our brothers and sisters, even our enemies. We learn to love others because we have been served by other people all of our lives, and we know that our success is tied to their success. We learn to love others because we identify with them in their pain, their struggles, and their joy, and we know that it is together as a community that we must strive for the establishment of God's kingdom. This kingdom is a spiritual kingdom, but it is also an incarnate one of loving acts, just laws, and effective, efficient, and fair institutions. Our role is to work on both the personal and institutional fronts for its coming because we know that good people create good laws and institutions, but also that good laws and institutions help to mold good people.

# PART II
## DOING GOOD PRACTICALLY

*"And let us consider how we may spur one another on toward love and good deeds."*
*—Hebrews 10:24*

# CHAPTER 10
## *DOING GOOD INDIVIDUALLY*

There are two main ways of doing good—individually and in cooperation with others. Some things we can do better by ourselves, and other things we can do better by working with other people, either informally or within formal associations. In this chapter, we will discuss some simple practical things that we can do on an individual basis.

When I was growing up, I liked to watch a TV program called "The Millionaire" in which an anonymous donor gave a million dollars in each weekly episode to a different individual facing a heart-wrenching problem. The money usually solved the problem, and everyone involved in the story, including us the TV spectators, came away with a feeling of satisfaction.

Unfortunately, in real life, very few people in the world have the financial resources to give a million dollars, or even a thousand dollars, to someone in order to help them solve their problems. However, we do have other resources at our disposal from which we can draw to make a positive contribution in the lives of others.

During his short life on earth, Jesus was very poor, yet he went about doing good, mostly on an individual basis and almost always without handing out money. He did it by touching, healing, admonishing, encouraging, and teaching. As part of his teachings, he told us that how we treated others, especially the most vulnerable in our societies, would be a criteria by which God would judge us. He also taught that we should give to anyone who asks of us. This particular instruction of Jesus is a very difficult standard and makes very little sense if we interpret it to mean that we should always give to someone exactly what he or she asks. Since those who ask us for help usually request money, we would very quickly become penniless if we did so. We would eventually become a burden rather than a blessing to others, and we even might be forced to beg ourselves. Perhaps, in some cases, such as in the Biblical story of the rich young ruler, or the story of St. Anthony of Egypt, selling all that we have and giving it to the poor is God's specific will for us. However, it is not necessarily so.

I believe that in his teaching us to give to everyone who asks, Jesus is calling us to give generously, but he is not necessarily telling us to give everyone exactly <u>what</u> they ask. Sometimes that would be impossible and at other times unwise. We need to consider first our possibilities, our responsibilities, our priorities, and our resources, as well as the real needs of those doing the asking.

It may be that we do not have in our possession what they ask, as was the case when the lame beggar asked Peter for alms outside the Temple. Peter replied that he had no silver or gold to give, but what he had, he would gladly give. He then touched the man, and the man got up and walked.

It may also be that we do have what the person requests, but we feel that giving it may not be for his or her good. For example, our children may want to do something fun, but we know it to be dangerous, so we withhold our permission. They may want an expensive gift, but we refuse it, because we want them to learn to earn their own money and thus understand its value. We also want them to grow up unselfish and unspoiled. The beggar may want our money, but we feel that he will not use it for what is good for him like food, clothes, transportation, or shelter, but rather for things that are harmful for him like alcohol and drugs. We may also feel that by giving money to beggars we may be encouraging them to be parasites or dishonest. What they ask for is not always what they really need or what is good for them in the long run.

Perhaps, though, the request we receive is legitimate, the cause is good, and we have the resources to fulfill the request. Still we might feel reluctant to give because we have other responsibilities and priorities for our money. Some of these might even be for our own personal benefit, such as our future medical needs and retirement. Some might be for the needs of those for whom we are responsible, like our young children or aging parents. Some might be for organizations to which we are committed, like our church or another non-governmental institution whose work we support.

God does not always give to us exactly what we ask for either, although he is abundantly benevolent and could easily do so. My belief is that he gives what is ultimately good for us, but not always what we want and perceive as good. Our role is to do the same with those who ask of us. While we may not have great financial resources, we each have many other gifts we can choose to give. Here are twenty-six of them that come to mind:

**Our attention:** It is a gift to others to recognize and pay attention to them. An act as simple as eye contact with a beggar confirms to them their worth. It is the bottom rung of the ladder of respect and empathy. An even better gift is to call someone by name and listen to them.

**A smile and a greeting:** This is another easy and beautiful bridge between friends and strangers. Smiles are contagious, often generating smiles in return. Barriers weaken in the face of a smile and greeting.

**A prayer:** A short silent prayer for people we see, wishing their good, places them in the care of an all-powerful and all-good God. Praying for someone makes us their advocates and helps us to see them as brothers and sisters of the same Father.

**Encouragement:** We all need to be encouraged. Encouragement can give us newfound strength to overcome deep despair. We are told to rejoice with those who rejoice and to mourn with those who mourn. Through solidarity and empathy, we learn to value the good of others as our own, and through encouragement, we help them fan the tiny embers of hope within themselves.

**Laughter:** "Laughter is the best medicine" is a common saying that often is true. We are not speaking, though, about mocking laughter that belittles others, but about the self-deprecating laughter that shares our own foibles with others. This kind of laughter produces a spirit of camaraderie.

**Time:** The gift of time is really an even more valuable gift than that of money. Time never can be recouped, whereas money can.

**Humility:** Humility is another good gift that we can give. Humility breaks down walls and gives a sense of worth to others. A self-deprecating joke on our part puts others at ease. Accepting advice and gifts with gratitude makes others feel bigger. Letting others have the spotlight and credit is a splendid and much appreciated gift that we can give.

**Forgiveness:** We all need forgiveness, not only from God, but also from others. Forgiveness is a gift that we can give, but it is not always easy to do so. Many times, we have been wronged and we may take a perverse kind of pleasure in remembering and recounting to others just how much we were wronged. We should recall that Jesus taught us that as we judge others, we will be judged, and as we forgive others, we shall be forgiven. That certainly puts things in perspective, since we all judge others and we all need forgiveness.

**Reconciliation:** Misunderstandings, prejudices, and differing interests create barriers between individuals and between organizations. Jesus calls us to unity and to be peacemakers and bridge builders whenever we can.

**Opportunities:** What we all want is a chance—a chance to prove ourselves, a chance to start over, a chance to speak, a chance to earn money. Giving someone such an opportunity is a special gift, and it might mean more to them than any other gift.

**A service:** We can provide people with a myriad of services. Some services, people request of us. Other services, it is we who see the need and offer our help spontaneously. In the home, we can help with daily chores like cleaning dishes and sweeping. We can help with transportation for the disabled, cooking for shut-ins, reading to those with visual problems. We can help by doing errands, babysitting, and fixing things. We can surprise others with notes of appreciation, with flowers or cookies, and with paying the parking meters for strangers. Opportunities are limitless.

**Sharing ourselves:** While some of us talk too much of ourselves, others of us hide our weaknesses and aspirations from others. It can be a blessing to others to take off our masks and to be vulnerable, sharing with them both our failings and our hopes.

**Counsel and knowledge:** We can counsel people by listening to them and giving them advice from our experience. We can teach them what we know. This can be in the form of helping them with homework, editing their writings, mentoring them, and coaching them in sports. We can volunteer to be a scout master, to teach a class, to share a recipe or some other special knowledge that we have that would benefit others.

**Contacts:** Networking is a great way to help people get the help they need. When we ourselves feel inadequate, we can refer to others those who come to us for help.

**Goods:** We can provide people with clothes, food, appliances, tools, vehicles, or other goods that they need.

**Politeness:** Some people see manners as formal and false, yet politeness is also a way of showing respect and kindness. Opening doors for others, allowing them preference, and addressing them with respect is a way of softening the harshness of much of our normal day-to-day lives.

**Visits:** Visiting people is a gift we can give. Such visits show that others mean something to us. This is especially important to someone who is grieving, is lonely, or in prison.

**Respect for the space of others:** On the other hand, it is important always to think first of the desires of others. Something that we might like, another might not. Sometimes visits might be a burden to a person, just as talking too long to a seat companion on the plane might not be what that person is wanting. One is reminded of the cartoon of the Boy Scout insisting on taking the little old lady across the street, even though that wasn't where she wanted to go! Smokers and people with loud radios, those who talk loud and long in public on their cell phones, those who party into the wee hours while others want rest, and churches with loud speakers blasting their messages into the streets, these do not respect the space of others.

**Blood and organ donations:** Such donations are gifts of life that we can give to others, usually at little sacrifice to ourselves.

**Personal hygiene:** This is another easy gift to give to others. We want to reach out and touch each other, but only with clean hands! Washed bodies, combed hair, brushed teeth, clean clothes, and the use of deodorant, are means by which we can become more pleasant companions to others.

**Beauty:** We all appreciate beauty and cleanliness in others and in our environment. Another important gift we can give is to pick up after others in the house, on the trails, and besides the road, or plant flowers and trees to make the world more beautiful for us all. A spouse can try to look the best he or she can, not out of vanity, but just to please their partner.

**Share a talent:** If we have special skills or talents, then we can share them with others. Music, painting, poetry, stories, photography, dance, and a host of other gifts, when shared, are universal up-lifters.

**Hospitality:** Providing hospitality to friends and to strangers is a great gift. Those of us who have lived in foreign countries or have settled in strange cities, know how grateful one is for the invitations that come one's way for food, lodging, outings, and friendship.

**Control of the tongue:** The tongue is both a source of good and evil. It can transmit information and laughter, but it can also offend with bragging, anger, negative opinions, and harsh and prejudiced jokes. One of the greatest gifts we give to others is to control our own tongues so that out of our mouths come forth blessings in the form of praise and encouragement, instead of curses, slander, and gossip. Our goal should be to speak the truth in love, and to be careful about both our words and the tones in which those words are delivered.

**Gratitude:** How thankful we should be for all the good that comes our way through grace. Our lives are filled with gifts from others that we take for granted. These include the neatly mowed yards that we pass and the trees planted along the road decades before. They include the voices of choirs, the years of medical training our doctors have had to undergo for our sake, the lonely work of writers who have shared their thoughts with us, our parents who have sacrificed for our good, friends who have helped us, and teachers who have taught us. The list of things to be grateful for has no end. One way of doing good to others and to ourselves is to thank all those who have helped us for their specific contributions to our happiness.

**Truth:** Truth is fundamental to healthy relationships. Valuing the truth makes us more humble and less likely to manipulate others. Telling the truth is a form of respect to others and a firm base on which to build a friendship. Sometimes silence is best, but if we do choose to speak, we should speak the truth, even though it makes us uncomfortable. We need to warn those we love of looming dangers when they make moral, economic, or social decisions that we feel will threaten their future well-being. Yet, truth-telling should always be coupled with the showing of love.

## HELPING OTHERS WITH MONEY

Most of these things we have listed above are non-monetary gifts that we can give to those who ask. However, the reality is that many people who ask us for something want money.

The Bible says that it is more joyful to give than to receive, but many of us do not feel that joy as much as we feel guilt, anxiety, and frustration when we think about giving money to others. Our guilt is because we know that we spend too much on ourselves and on our families and that we do not give enough to others. Our anxiety is because we feel that our supply of money is very limited and may not be enough to meet our present and future needs. Our frustration is that there are so many causes to give to, that many of the people who ask us for money are manipulating us, and that our gift will not be used as represented.

**How then can we give money with less anxiety and frustration and with more joy?** As with all other aspects of doing good, the first and most important step to increase our generosity and our joy in giving is to grow in our love of God. As we learn to love him, we will learn to trust him for our needs, for direction, and for forgiveness, even when we fail as badly as the wastrel son in Jesus' parable does. With such a trust come security, peace, generosity, and joy. Here are some other aides to changing our attitudes to giving:

We need to realize that all things are God's. We are just the stewards of them for a very short time. We all die and we cannot take our properties and toys with us. As a preacher once said, when the game is over, all the money, property, and pieces go back into the Monopoly box, and the scoreboard is erased.

We have to learn how to be good stewards of what we have while we have it. God wants us to enjoy what he has given us, but he also wants us to be wise in its use. From the parable of the talents, we learn that he wants us to multiply his gifts to us. We also know from the Bible that he wants us to be generous in sharing those gifts with others, starting with our family and kin, but continuing out to strangers and even enemies. He wants us to use those gifts to help others and not to hurt them. (For example, giving money to individual beggars without knowing their background may not be wise, especially if adequate government or non-governmental organizations and programs are in place to help them. If they are in place, then it might be wiser to support the beggar through the programs.)

Contrary to what we might expect, when we give to God and to others, we receive back more than we give—often in this life, but always in the world to come, according to the promise of Jesus. As the proverbial expression states, "what goes around, comes around."

Another way to change our attitude is to recognize that we are selfish people and mostly slaves of material things. To break out of our bondage to ourselves and to things is a life-long learning process. Only gradually do we learn to become more generous and less fearful, and to be more humble and less ostentatious about giving. In Appendix 2 of this book, I have outlined some questions we might ask ourselves to help us to become more generous and wise in our giving. It is useful to think through what we have to give, and how, why, and to whom we are to give it.

As to what portion of our wealth we should give to others, Jews and Christians are encouraged in their faith tradition to start at 10% of their income as a base guide for religious and charitable giving. Muslims use 2.5% of one's net worth as their guide. Some people decide that they are able to give much more. Some people even say that we should give until it hurts. A very generous Christian friend of mine, however, had a better idea. He said that he gave until it felt good!

How we use our charitable and religious "tithe" differs from person to person. In the Bible we are taught to use our gifts to support our religious leaders, to spread the good news of the gospel, to help the sick, the poor, the lonely, the disabled, widows and orphans, and all who are vulnerable. We are taught to be hospitable to strangers and to be good stewards of our world. Some of our gifts we can designate for organizations and others for individuals; some we can use for proactive giving and some we can designate for unexpected requests. But in all of our giving, we should try our best to give wisely so our gifts are used effectively and efficiently to do good, not harm.

# A PRAYER FOR EACH DAY

Each day as we prepare for our tasks and encounters with others, it is useful to remember constantly that we are all children of the same

Father. All the people that we will meet this day are therefore our brothers and sisters. Just as in any healthy family where one member understands and feels pain in the sufferings of another member, so we should feel pain in the sufferings of those we meet today. Just as one member feels happiness in the success of another member, so should we rejoice in the accomplishments of others. Why should we envy them? Their talents as bakers, artists, athletes, writers, entertainers, truck drivers, farmers, administrators, etc. benefit us and therefore should bring us pleasure.

It is also useful to remember the truth that all of us at different times in our lives are sometimes beggars and are sometimes givers. From time-to-time, we all find ourselves in situations when we need the help of other people or in situations when we can give help. Since we owe so much to each other for our own survival and happiness, it is natural that we should want to return the favor to them or to "pass it on" to others.

A good desire to have as we start each new day is the desire to grow in our love for God and for others. A good prayer to accompany that desire is the prayer of Saint Francis of Assisi:

*"Lord, make me an instrument of your peace.*
*Where there is hatred, let me sow love;*
*where there is injury, pardon;*
*where there is doubt, faith;*
*where there is despair, hope;*
*where there is darkness, light;*
*and where there is sadness, joy.*
*O Divine Master, grant that I may not so much seek*
*to be consoled as to console;*
*to be understood as to understand;*
*to be loved as to love.*
*For it is in giving that we receive;*
*it is in pardoning that we are pardoned;*
*and it is in dying that we are born to eternal life."*

# CHAPTER 11
## *DOING GOOD WITH OTHERS*

As we have seen in the last chapter, there is much good we can do by ourselves with little organizing or fanfare. Small individual acts of kindness throughout the day in our families and in our encounters with others can ease problems and bring happiness.

There are numerous other problems, however, whose size and complexity demand the cooperation of many individuals in order to solve them. On an informal basis, friends and strangers join together to push a stalled car out of traffic; they fill sandbags to help fellow citizens threatened by a flood; they organize themselves to build a house for a needy person; they prepare and distribute food for a community event; they pool money so that a sick friend can have an operation. There are a myriad of ways that we cooperate informally to do good. In my experience, women are particularly adept at thinking of ways to help others and then teaming together to do it in an informal way.

Sometimes, the problems that confront us are too major to be resolved informally. We must apply concentrated and continuous effort over longer stretches of time and involve more people and resources in order to deal with them. We need to determine goals and strategies, establish organizations, hire employees, pay salaries, purchase equipment, and rent or construct buildings. Again, from my experience, men seem to be more attracted to these more formal ways of helping through organizations. We can classify these formal organizations in many ways, but one of the broadest is to identify them either as governmental or non-governmental organizations.

We establish governments in order to preserve the peace, to protect the life and property of citizens, and to perform many other useful and necessary functions in a society. Governments usually join with other governments in alliances. Municipal governments are a part of state governments; state governments are a part of national governments; and national governments join in alliances with other national governments to promote such issues as trade, security, health, human rights, food production, emergency relief, protection of the environment, and cultural preservation. The United Nations is the prime example of such an alliance of governments.

Besides governments, a vast number of non-governmental organizations exist throughout the world to carry out different missions, mostly for the good. We may classify them in various ways, but perhaps the central way in which they differ one from the other is based on whether or not they are designed to make money for their organizers. "For-profit organizations" are businesses that seek to increase their profits and then distribute them to their owners and shareholders. "Not-for-profit organizations" also try to increase their income, but they channel excess revenues back into the organization and do not distribute them to their shareholders. In theory, not-for-profit organizations are "owned" by the communities they serve and not by specific individuals.

Organizations differ among themselves in many other ways as well. Some organizations are local, while others are national or international. Some organizations have small budgets of a few hundred dollars and others have budgets of billions of dollars. Some serve only their own membership, while others offer their services to the general public or target specific groups such as children, social minorities, and the economically deprived. Some are democratic and inclusive in the way they are organized and run, while others are more authoritarian and paternalistic.

Organizations also differ greatly in the types of products and services they offer. Some manufacture a wide range of products and others offer services. One can find an organization for just about any interest category—animal rights, human rights, sports, peace, stamp collecting, health concerns, economic development, and the protection of the environment, just to name a few.

The more one deals with organizations, the more one finds that they behave in ways similar to individuals. This is because they are made-up of people like you and me. Like individuals, organizations can have mixed motivations and struggle with ethical questions. As they seek to do good, they can also be selfish and competitive. They measure success not only by how well they fulfill their mission and accomplish their service goals, but also by how much power, money, and influence they have and how they rank in relationship to other organizations with similar missions. Like individuals, they tout their glories and try to hide their defects, and their successes and failures reflect on us, their members. While we may discourage individual pride, we usually accept and promote institutional and national pride as positive and good. Just look at how we cheer for our schools' and our cities' sports teams!

Organizations play crucial roles in all of our lives. It is in our organizations that we interact with others and become involved in concerns bigger than ourselves. Our sense of identity and of self-worth are often determined in a large part by these organizations with which we are identified—by our families, our schools and universities, our churches, social and service clubs, businesses, political parties, and nations. Many of our friends, life experiences, and attitudes come from our involvement in these organizations, and they are one of the principal means by which we try to do good in the world. This has certainly been true in my case and it is why others have encouraged me to share with you here my own personal organizational experience. It is on this experience that rests many of the observations in the rest of this book.

For most of my adult life, I have tried to do good mostly with and through the non-governmental and U.N. organizations with which I have been affiliated. After graduating from Davidson College in 1967 (including a year of study in France), I won a Fulbright grant and taught English and American literature in an Indian government university and traveled throughout the country doing research on similarities in Hindu and Christian mysticism. It was at the Hindu holy site of Rishikesh that I saw close-up the deformities, poverty, and hopelessness of people with leprosy for the first time and determined in my heart that one day I would try to do something to help people with this ancient and misunderstood disease.

In 1968-1970, I worked for almost a year and a half with UNICEF in Vietnam during the height of the Vietnam War. At first, my job was to help coordinate the building of hospital wards for civilian burn and maternity cases in Danang and Saigon. Afterwards, I became the UNICEF field representative for the northern provinces of South Vietnam, and my job expanded to work together with the South Vietnamese Social Welfare Ministry to set up feeding programs for 10,000 children in refugee camps outside of Danang, Hue, and Quang Ngai. I also helped organize the delivery of U.N. emergency supplies to numerous Vietnamese communities (including a leprosy settlement) that had been attacked or been the victim of other disasters. This experience brought home to me the high cost, terrible destruction, intense suffering, and dehumanization caused by war.

Returning to the United States at the end of 1970 to face trial in Montgomery, Alabama for my refusal to join the U.S. armed forces (for which I was acquitted), I worked as a psychiatric aide at the Yale University Psychiatric Institute. During this period, I finished a master's degree in public health at the same University. During my studies at Yale, I received a scholarship to fund six months of thesis research in Tanzania on the needs of people with Hansen's disease (leprosy). Of particular interest to me were the questions of how we could overcome the strong stigma of the disease and better promote the social and economic integration of people affected by it.

After graduating from the Yale program, I married the daughter of Christian missionaries whose grandparents had founded in Costa Rica the "Latin America Mission" and its many institutions—hospital, orphanage, school, seminary, radio station, etc. We moved to Spain in 1973 for my new wife, Clare, to finish her Masters in Spanish literature. While living in Madrid, I received an invitation by the American Leprosy Missions, the Pan American Health Organization (PAHO), and the Government of Brazil for me to do a similar study in Brazil to the one I had done in Tanzania. At the time, there were some 600,000 persons affected by Hansen's disease (leprosy) in Brazil.

I accepted, and after three months of visiting leprosy programs in Venezuela, my wife and I moved to Brazil where we would spend most of the next fifteen years. The first few years of our stay were oriented towards researching the obstacles that prevented the social integration of people affected by Hansen's disease, and in proposing a plan to overcome those obstacles. The plan, designed with the help of my Brazilian colleagues, I called *PRO-REHAB*.

*PRO-REHAB*, once it was approved by Brazilian government authorities and international supporters, required work on many fronts at the same time: It involved the setting-up of training programs and the transformation of leprosaria, leprosy clinics, and leprosy settlements into integrated and non-stigmatizing institutions that offered a full range of services to people with Hansen's disease and other problems. It involved, too, the designing and founding of local and national not-for-profit vocational rehabilitation centers for all types of disabled persons under the name of *SORRI*, which I then directed.

I was also a co-founder of local and national organizations of disabled persons. One of them, *MORHAN*, led by a friend disabled by Hansen's disease, now has dozens of branches throughout Brazil and has had an important impact on Hansen's disease work both in Brazil and in other countries. Other work in Brazil included helping to found the first graduate course for vocational rehabilitation counselors in Brazil and a month as a PAHO consultant to the Ministry of Health in Brasilia.

My time in Brazil, and taking off a year in 1984 to attend and graduate from the "Institute for Not-for-Profit Management" at Columbia University and the "Advanced Management Program" at Harvard Business School, taught me a lot. I learned about business and NGOs, research methods, grass-root organizing, setting up not-for-profits and small businesses within them, working with governments and international agencies, dealing with prejudices, adapting to different cultures, and the importance of listening to the people we are trying to help.

At a new invitation from the Board of the American Leprosy Missions, I became ALM president in 1989, and then in 1994 became president of ILEP, the International Federation of Anti-Leprosy Organizations based in London. ILEP was a federation then of 22 world organizations with work in about 100 countries These experiences gave me much insight into the politics and the fundraising aspects of doing good and the importance of diplomacy and of cooperation within and between organizations.

After my time as ILEP president was up, and I had written and published a book on the social aspects of leprosy work called <u>Don't Treat Me Like I Have Leprosy</u>, I decided to fulfill a life-long dream and write a novel. I published <u>The Descendant</u> in 2002. During this writing time, I also did some consulting with a few organizations in Great Britain, Central America, and the United States.

Towards the end of 2002, I accepted my brother-in-law's invitation to help him and some of his very successful Central American business friends, set up a small economic development program in Nicaragua. We called the program *Adelante,* and concentrated our efforts on the very poor, but very beautiful, San Juan River region of the country. *Adelante*'s main aim was to encourage eco-tourism as an economic motor for the region. In order to achieve this goal, we focused on a number of different activities. One was to bring together business competitors to try to solve problems that they all were facing. We also established a sister-city relationship between the region's capital and an American town with the same name, tried to improve tourist related services in the area by giving small and medium sized loans to hotels, restaurants, owners of boats, and internet cafes. Other activities included sponsoring small training seminars, printing brochures, lobbying for airstrips, better roads, and more official entry points with Costa Rica, sponsoring fairs so that local artisans could sell their goods in Managua, the capital, and doing whatever else seemed important to attracting tourists to the region. This three-year experience gave me considerable insight into the potential, but also the many problems of economic development programs, both small and large.

At present, I am now mostly back in the United States, volunteering, participating on the board of Warren Wilson College, still writing, still involved in small ways in *Adelante* and *SORRI,* and am now planning with my wife a possible spiritual retreat and training center on our farm in Brazil. I am also still struggling with how to be and do good better, and I am still learning from those who are more natural at it than I am.

I look back now with gratitude at all of the people and organizations with whom and with which I have been identified throughout my life. (I have also been fortunate to have in my extended family many relatives who have served as ministers, doctors, social workers, nurses, teachers, volunteers, founders of corporations, important government officials, executives and board members of international NGOs and businesses.) All of these persons and the organizations with which I have been associated have encouraged me, taught me, and provided me with the tools and structure I needed for accomplishing the good that I set out to do. As a lone individual, I could never have succeeded. Working together with others in organizations greatly expands our effectiveness.

Because governmental and non-governmental organizations are so important to us in our efforts to do good, we will now consider in a little more detail how they work and our possible roles within them.

# CHAPTER 12
## *DOING GOOD THROUGH GOVERNMENT*

When one talks of doing good in an organized way, one's first thoughts probably turn to government. Most people would likely agree that the main purpose of government is to promote the common good of its citizens in some of the following basic ways:

**Providing security:** The world is a jungle of competing individual and group interests. A primary function of government is therefore to provide protection from external threats for the people living under its jurisdiction.

**Rule making:** Another of the main functions of a government is to promote order by making the rules by which the people within its boundaries live and function. These rules are usually in the form of a written constitution and secondary codes of laws based on that constitution.

**Rule enforcing:** Rule enforcement is also a function of a government through its monitoring, policing, and judicial systems. Sometimes governments use positive reinforcement through tax incentives and other rewards to keep people in line. Most often, however, governments use negative disincentives to make people obey laws for the common good. These go from societal disapproval, official reprimands, and monetary fines, to prison and even execution in many countries.

**Economic well-being:** Governments have a central role in promoting the economic well-being of their citizens. Governments control interest rates, taxes, the printing of currency, the rules of trade, labor laws, and in some countries, they control strategic industries and services and heavily subsidize others. They build highways, ports, subways, and airports so that goods and people can move quickly. They are bulk buyers of services and promote research and training to create new products and jobs.

**Social well-being:** Governments also promote the social well-being of their citizens. They are heavily involved in creating and maintaining educational, health, and welfare systems for their people. Governments sponsor fire departments and libraries and they support the arts and a host of useful social services through grants. They have programs to assist the poor, the jobless, the old, the handicapped, the mentally ill, and many other groups without alternate means of support. They also legislate to protect minorities as the makeup of our populations has become increasingly diverse with the influx of people of different races, cultures, and religions.

**Sense of dignity, freedom, happiness, and pride:** Successful governments are those that promote the good of their people through other less material ways as well. They instill a sense of belonging, of pride, and of dignity in their people through a shared history, emphasizing the noble and the good. Recognizing individual differences and needs, they guarantee individual freedom so that people are allowed to seek happiness and fulfillment in their own ways, so long as these ways do not interfere with the rights of others.

**Preparation for the future:** A good government is one that not only leads a country in the present, but also lays groundwork for the future prosperity and happiness of its citizens. It protects a people's water supplies, air, land, and fauna. It seeks ways to sustain a good life for future generations by wise laws, by education and health norms, by research, by establishing stable and effective institutions, and by promoting peace with other nations.

Governments are the biggest, most powerful, and richest of the organizations with which we will probably be associated during our lifetimes. Within any government, there are dozens of sectors and thousands of jobs where we can do good as lawmakers, teachers, social workers, health workers, police officers, administrators, planners, counselors, inspectors, etc. We can do good both to those we serve and also to those with whom we work. To some philosophers, the role of a public servant in government is the highest calling to which we can aspire.

# PUBLIC SERVANTS

Public servants include both those hired to do a job within government and those who are elected to the positions that they hold. As most of the world's governments today are now some sort of representative democracy, their legislators and their principal executive leaders usually are elected and not appointed.

It takes a strong person to run for high public office—not only because of the personal scrutiny and attacks that one has to endure from the press and from those competing for the same position, but also because of the temptations that one faces in the process of getting to office and staying in office. Among such temptations are the desire for personal power, the urge to be well-liked and admired by all, the lust for personal economic gain, the idea that one is above common morality, and the mentality that the end justifies the means. Unfortunately, in many countries of the world, government officials are more feared and disdained than loved and admired because so many of them cannot resist the temptations of their office and use their positions more to help themselves than to serve others.

Once elected or appointed to leadership positions, a person in office who sincerely desires to serve others has to ponder some very difficult questions. Here are just two of them:

**To whom should one be primarily answerable?** To whom does one owe one's first allegiance as one makes decisions about policies, laws, and the allocation of resources? Should it be to the nation as a whole, to those one represents geographically, to one's political party, to one's family, tribe, or religion, to one's financial supporters, to one's personal desires and needs, to one's personal conscience, or to God?

People come down on different sides in this question. Some put personal interests above everything else. Some put political party or local loyalties before national loyalties. Some put individual principles, conscience, or what they consider God's will first. Ethical candidates for office should understand well their own personal hierarchy of values and accountability before running for a position and be open about them in their campaigns for election.

My own belief is that a public servant's first loyalty must be to the highest values he or she can imagine. Many people, including myself, call those values God or God's will. Some prefer to call them principles like justice, truth, mercy, or the good of humankind.

I believe that the next highest loyalty on the list should be the vows one makes on taking office to obey and uphold the laws of the land and to fulfill the promises that the candidate made while in his or her campaign for office. Our leaders should keep their word or explain carefully to those who voted for them what new facts caused them to change their minds.

In cases where there are clear conflicts of interests, I believe that the public servant should choose the higher principle and the greater good over the lesser. To my way of thinking, this means that human rights are above a nation's rights; and a nation's rights above state, party, and institutional rights.

**When should one compromise and when should one not?** Compromise is another dilemma that our leaders face. Sometimes it is good to compromise because compromise shows that we are considering the needs, interests, and attitudes of others as well as our own. Isn't that what "loving others as ourselves" means? It is also good to compromise because that is the only way that a democracy can survive and work. Do not philosophers tell us that moderation between two extremes is the path that leads to well-being?

There are times, however, when it is wrong to compromise. This is the case when fundamental issues are at stake that involve basic beliefs, matters of life and death, or when compromise is done for purely selfish reasons.

Government officials have many opportunities for service and for doing good that others do not have, but as we have said, they also have many temptations to corruption and pride that others do not have. If one is to be a force for the good in government, then one must constantly be aware of these temptations and reject them.

# ORDINARY CITIZENS

Even if we ourselves never seek a position as a government employee, we also have important roles to play in government as ordinary citizens. One of our duties as citizens is to prevent abuses by our leaders through personal vigilance and by supporting transparency, legal checks and balances, and a free press. Another role we have as ordinary citizens is to participate in putting good and wise people into office by our votes, volunteering, and finances. We, the citizens, are the ones who are responsible for the governments that represent us at the local, regional, and national levels.

Like "public servants," those of us who are ordinary citizens also sometimes face conflicts of interests and hard choices in our relationship to government. For example, when there is disagreement between local and national governments, to which of these do we owe our final loyalty? Usually the answer today is to nation, but many wars and trials revolve around people giving other answers to this question. Remember, for example the anguish of Robert E. Lee as he tried to decide if he would accept the command of the U.S. Armies offered to him, or the command of the Army of Virginia, his home state.

Another major issue that many citizens face is whether they should always submit to the will of the government expressed through its laws, even if they disagree strongly with some of those laws for moral reasons. Normally, we submit to laws because they are seen as just, established for the good of all, and because they are the foundation of order and peace in any democratic state. Even in those cases when we do not happen to agree with a law, we most often obey it out of fear of punishment or because we are guided by slogans like "my country, right or wrong."

At times, however, individuals believe that certain governmental policies are so wrong that they cannot obey them. They therefore oppose them in word and in action. Some persons, like Ghandi and Martin Luther King Jr., take the road of passive resistance to what they consider unjust laws. They are willing to be imprisoned or to die for what they believe, but they are not willing to kill others for their beliefs. They prefer peace of conscience before life and physical freedom, and they hope that their example will persuade others to join them in their campaign for justice.

Other individuals feel that controlled violence and killing are sometimes necessary and ethical alternatives to what they consider evil or unjust laws. This was the view of the Christian theologian Dietrich Bonhoeffer who plotted to assassinate Hitler during World War II. It was the view of some Latin American priest revolutionaries who took up arms against what they thought were unjust governments. It is also the view of soldiers of every nation who have gone to battle against their government's enemies in what they believe are "just wars." While they might believe that it is wrong to kill people, they also believe that killing sometimes must be done in self-defense and for the promotion of some higher good.

Personally, I have always struggled with these dilemmas, and sometimes I have come down on one side and then on another. Like many people of my generation who faced the Vietnam draft, I was against the draft and the war. Most of my reasons for being against the draft were selfish. I did not want to go to Vietnam because I had better things to do with my life. I did not want to be ordered around in the military, and most of all, I did not want to die!

Yet, there were other more noble reasons as well for being against the war. Mainly, I did not want to kill a fellow human being. Life is precious, and killing to me was an absolute action and was being done in Vietnam for a relative and imperfect political reason. I was unaware of any war where all the right and good was arrayed on one side, and all the wrong and injustice was on the other. Vietnam was certainly not one of them. I did not believe that we should be involved in a Vietnamese civil war, and I did not want to kill someone's father, son, or brother for an always-changing political reason. I reasoned that the Vietnamese, like the Germans and Japanese who were once our enemies, would one day become our friends. Why should I cause such sorrow to them and pain to my own conscience by taking life? Anyway, I knew that killing promotes more killing, and vengeance, more vengeance. In that way, destruction spreads like a tsunami. I also knew that in any assassination attempt, war, or revolution, people make mistakes and the innocent die. Were the "victories" of war really worth it all?

Yet, another part of my reason and conscience called me to duty to my country, to overcome my cowardliness, to uphold the freedoms that I hold dear, and to not be a fool and let unopposed communism conquer the world. I knew that others, who also did not want to die, overcame their fears and joined the armed forces out of duty and principle. They felt that they were defending ideals that were worth dying and killing for. Why should I get out of facing the same dangers they faced while believing another way?

My own personal solution to this dilemma was a compromise. I decided to refuse military service because I did not want to be part of a killing machine in Vietnam, but I also decided to go to Vietnam as a UNICEF volunteer helping in relief and refugee work. But while I felt noble because I too faced danger, yet carried no gun, the truth is that I depended on the guns of others to protect me, on the transport of the armed forces to deliver our emergency goods, and on the food and donated supplies of my country to help those in need. In the end, therefore, was I really better than anyone else?

The difficulty of being ethically consistent has been even more evident to me in recent years as I have struggled with my own opinion about the right thing for the United States to do in Afghanistan and Iraq, our new international battle grounds. Although the loss of human life and other horrors of war should keep us from any war, I did support in my mind the U.N. sanctioned invasion of Afghanistan as it seemed reasonable to me as a police action to maintain international law. On the other hand, I opposed the initial invasion of Iraq by the U.S. and its allies, because I felt that our attacks there were aggressive and not defensive in nature and that our nation did not have the full backing of the U.N. as it did in the invasion of Afghanistan.

Yet, once we were in Iraq, I found myself modifying my views about our presence there. While it might have been wrong to go in, I came to think that it would be morally irresponsible to leave the country before a reasonably strong and just government had been set up to maintain the peace and to promote the good of the people. We broke it, and therefore we must help fix it! The same was true for Afghanistan.

Both countries have since held free elections and the officials they have elected have asked for at least some U.S. troops to stay. Therefore, I feel that our continued presence is now justified until the elected governments of Afghanistan and Iraq ask us to leave. The stakes are too high to do otherwise. In my view, a unilateral precipitated withdrawal would be disastrous to the majority of the people in these countries as chaos and even more destruction would ensue. Such a withdrawal would also encourage the spread of an ideology that seems evil to me, an ideology that uses terror of the innocent to force its beliefs on others. While it is terrible to kill the innocent accidentally in a military action, it is pure evil to target intentionally the innocent as part of a military and political strategy.

I share this personal example to illustrate how difficult it is for a person to come to clear-cut ethical decisions about the actions of governments in wars. So much is at stake in a war—human freedom, human suffering, and human wealth—both our own and that of others. Because so much is at stake, we as citizens need to make sure that our leaders do not lead us into such adventures without first struggling with all of the issues. It is so easy to be wrong.

As ordinary citizens of our nations, we also must face daily other moral and political issues in which the individual freedoms and values that we hold so dearly clash with one another. Some of these issues are clearly matters of life or death like war, the death penalty, euthanasia, suicide, abortion, gun control, and safety laws for drugs, medicines, food, and other products. Others are justice issues, such as the respect for individual freedoms, the ending of extreme poverty, and the treatment of the weak and minorities of all types. Other issues involve quality of life, like the use of natural resources and the protection of the environment, job creation, housing, the subsidy of the arts, and the control of pornography. We agonize over these issues because they are rarely black and white.

Most citizens love their countries and are proud of them. For example, I am very grateful for being a United States citizen. I like that we are a democracy and that we have all kinds of freedoms, but especially religious freedom, so that people have the liberty to believe and worship as they will. A forced belief to me is an absurdity and a violation of God's will and of human rights. I like that in theory, and mostly in practice, that no one in America is above the law and that even the powerful and influential have to face their day in court if they have done something wrong. I like the openness of our society and the ability to move upward socially and around geographically. I like that we are a generous nation of volunteers and givers, people helping people. I like that we are a diverse nation and that people from all over the world have found opportunities here. I like that we are a nation of problem solvers. I like that our founders were, for the most part, decent and intelligent men who had a strong belief in human rights and in the Creator who bestowed those rights.

Like the citizens of most countries, I do not like other things about my nation and I would like to change them. I do not like that we are sometimes heavy-handed in the way we treat other countries, often exploiting them for our own political and economic gain. I do not like that we are so wasteful, spending so much of the world's resources on so few people. I do not like that we are so litigious, seeking opportunities to make a quick buck at someone else's expense, rather than seeking real justice. I do not like that we often seem to be a country of whiners and victims, always blaming others for our problems and expecting our government to protect us from all harm. I do not like how fame, money, and sex seem more important than individuals and moral values to so many people. I do not like our "gotcha" society of negative campaigning and an egotistical media that seems always out to show the worst. I do not like our high crime rate and huge prison population and the mass of weapons available for people to kill each other. I do not like that we allow the death of children in selfish abortions, and that we still have the death penalty for some crimes.

So what should we do as citizens who love our countries, but also recognize the faults of those countries? We must work to reform them. Just as we aspire to be good and do good as individuals, we should also strive to make our governments as good as we can make them. We want them to be effective and efficient, but we also want them to be just—both in their dealings with the citizens under their jurisdiction, as well as with other governments, even those that we temporarily perceive as enemies. For a society to function, we have to balance our own individual freedoms with those of others. For a world to function, we have to balance our own national freedoms and rights with those of others.

Even though our first duty is to try to reform ourselves, I feel it is wrong to be isolationists. Our goals as individuals and government should be to create a better world, and not just a better corner of that world. After all, we are all inter-dependent and we all share the same earth, water, and air. We cannot put blinders on and not be concerned about the pollution, poverty, and violation of human rights around the world. The policies of one country affect people in other countries. We should want all peoples to live in the best societies possible, and we need to work humbly together towards that goal. One of our main tools for doing that is our super-national organizations.

## SUPER-NATIONAL ORGANIZATIONS

More than ever, international agencies, representing the national governments that are their members, have become very important for the world's security and its economic and social progress. These agencies try to promote peace, balance national interests, defend human rights, diminish poverty and sickness, promote culture, and protect the environment.

The United Nations is the most important international organization in the world today in terms of membership and impact. Under the umbrella of the United Nations are some of the most active and significant agencies in the world. While all of these are political in nature, representing the interests of member governments, they also do a lot of good in health, the environment, arms control, refugees, children, agriculture, commerce, money lending, promoting culture and human rights, and in defending the interests of at-risk populations.

The issues that the U.N. deals with are very complex, and the resources and liberty of action that it has for dealing with them are quite inadequate. Part of the reason for this inadequacy is that rich and powerful nations of the U.N. do not want to lower their own standards of living or relinquish their own power and prestige in their efforts to help poorer nations. Another part of the reason is that countries have different ways of looking at the same issues and unified action is not easy. One country may support an action because they view the action as protecting a human right. Another country may oppose the same action because they view it as undermining national sovereignty and disrespecting one's culture.

Doing good through governments and super-national organizations therefore is sometimes difficult. We should not give up hope, however. Underlying all of our governments and cultures is a basic moral code that unites us all. In our hearts, we know that all men and women are our brothers and sisters, and truth, justice, wisdom, courage, moderation, and mercy are values on which we can all agree. The existence of the "Universal Declaration of Human Rights" is a proof of that.

# CHAPTER 13
## *DOING GOOD THROUGH NON-GOVERNMENTAL ORGANIZATIONS*

Besides governments and super-national organizations, another tool we have for collectively doing good are our non-governmental organizations—NGOs. Less formal, smaller, and more agile than governments and usually more attuned to individual and local interests, non-governmental agencies have had an enormous impact on our lives and on our world. There are millions of such organizations around the world. Although the term "NGO" today usually refers to not-for-profit organizations, for-profit organizations are also non-governmental organizations.

## *FOR-PROFIT ORGANIZATIONS*

For-profit organizations, or businesses, like General Electric or Sam's Auto Shop, provide goods and services for the public, jobs for employees, income for suppliers, taxes for local, state, and national governments, profit for owners, and sometimes very important donations for not-for-profits. They are the cornerstone of the economic life of a community and nation.

There are many ways of doing good in for-profit organizations. Businesses do good by providing products and services of good quality that are safe, fairly priced, marketed in a transparent and truthful way, and that are guaranteed in some fashion. Employees do good by supporting the business and their fellow employees with their labor, their ideas, their allegiance, and their commitment to excellence. Business owners do good by providing jobs, paying fair wages, obeying labor laws, treating workers with respect, making the working experience as enjoyable as possible, and involving the employees in some way in the decision-making process. They also do good by obeying commercial laws, protecting the environment, and finding ways to support activities which benefit the community, including financial assistance to not-for-profit organizations. The taxes that they pay are a substantial part of the fuel that runs our governments. While one cannot overestimate the importance of for-profit organizations in doing good, our attention in the rest of this chapter will be on the not-for-profit organization.

## *NOT-FOR-PROFIT ORGANIZATIONS*

Not-for-profit organizations' primary purpose for existing is to meet some community need. Since they are not profit oriented, in order to survive and continue their work, they depend on voluntary contributions of money, goods, labor, and services from the community as well as tax exemptions and grants from the government. Not-for-profit organizations relieve suffering and promote the interests of the poor by providing basic health and social services. They are also involved in education, religion, culture, the environment, community development and a host of other activities, sometimes only locally, but other times internationally.

In any major community, one can find dozens of examples of not-for-profit organizations. People of similar beliefs want to worship together, so they form a church; others want to have a safe, instructive, and fun environment for their children, so they join together to form scout troops, private schools, and Little League sports teams. Still others want to protect their homes, so they establish volunteer fire departments or neighborhood watch groups. Persons who want to promote culture found symphony orchestras, museums, and theater and dance groups. Those who wish to enjoy and protect the environment of their community often organize nature clubs to create trails and parks, pick up trash, protect water supplies, and lobby for protective laws. Those who have a particular concern for the sick, the poor, the lonely, and the oppressed, may establish community health programs, food banks, orphanages, assisted living homes, and many other helpful organizations. Sometimes, wealthy individuals, wanting to "give back" to their communities, create foundations into which they deposit millions of their dollars to help finance all of the above.

We join and work together in not-for-profit agencies for many reasons. One is to solve or diminish problems. Another is to generate the good feelings and sense of self-worth that come from helping and working together with others in a good cause. Still another is to fulfill our sense of duty to our community. Sometimes we gain financial advantages from our association with not-for-profits in the form of tax deductions. At other times, we also gain personal recognition—from simple "thank-you" notes to plaques and buildings named in our honor or in the honor of those we love.

While governments have much greater resources and zones of action than not-for-profits, not-for-profits have several advantages over governments. Perhaps the primary advantages they have are the freedom to try new approaches to solving problems, to give to whom they like without red tape or delay, to hire and fire with less outside interference, and to meet needs that others are not meeting. Eventually, governments take over many of the services initiated by not-for-profit organizations.

Both not-for-profit and for-profit organizations are usually started by visionary entrepreneurs who see a need, but also an opportunity for meeting the need. These social entrepreneurs are problem solvers, and their ability to identify problems and bring together people to help deal with them is a major force in our progress as a civilization. There are so many problems that need solving, and so many things that we can do to make life more safe and enjoyable.

Working with a not-for-profit is a highly fulfilling way of doing good. Because there are so many good causes in the world and our time and resources are limited, we should choose carefully the organizations with which we want to become involved. Advocates for different causes and organizations constantly bombard us with pleas for our time, talents, and financial help. To whom should we say "yes?" With which causes and organizations should we become involved and to what extent? Should we contribute a little money or a lot? Should we volunteer to help-out only in some small tasks and events, or should we offer to become a board member, a full time volunteer, or employee? Should we help start a not-for-profit ourselves?

## Choosing our causes

In choosing the causes that we will support, it is useful to consider first our own interests and needs. As a father or mother of young children, we may feel it wise to become involved in organizations like the scouts, the church, the PTA, and the Little League. These are particularly important at this time of our lives and that of our children. We may also remember the personal benefits that we have received in the past from such groups and decide to repay them in some positive way with donations of time and money. We may also want to honor a friend or a family member by supporting organizations that interested or helped them. Of course, we may want to assist organizations just because they do a good job in dealing with an important problem.

Sometimes, it may be that there are no local organizations meeting the need that we feel need targeting. In this case, we can try to get an existing not-for-profit to expand their array of services or clientele to include the needed services. If that is not possible, then we may decide to join with others to start a new not-for-profit to meet the need. This happened to me in Brazil in the 1970s. Unable to convince existing disability or job training organizations to offer their services to people disabled by Hansen's disease (leprosy), I had to create a new organization that served all the disabled, including those affected by Hansen's disease. Starting and maintaining a not-for-profit, however, means a huge commitment of time and energy.

# Choosing our role in the organization

Once we choose what organizations to support, we then must consider what role we would like to have in the organization. Some organizational roles involve much more time, effort, and finances than others. We might elect to take on the heavier responsibilities of a board member or employee, or opt for the lesser burden of being a short-time volunteer helping out with stuffing envelopes or answering the phone. We might choose to be a major donor over a long time span, or a one-time giver of a few dollars. Whatever role we choose, we need to have a clear understanding of what is required of us. Many unfortunate conflicts happen within organizations because of misunderstandings about the duties and time commitments of its supporters.

As volunteers or employees, our chief responsibility is to make sure that the organization we are involved with fulfills its mission in an effective, efficient, and ethical manner. We should come to meetings on time, treat others with courtesy and respect, listen well and offer ideas, give time and money, know and respect the lines of authority in place, and perform the duties that we have agreed to perform. Just because we are volunteers does not mean that we have the freedom to shirk the responsibilities that we have assumed. Our goal is to help and not to be a burden to the organization. Whatever role we choose to accept, we should try to fulfill it as conscientiously as possible.

# Understanding the organization

As supporters of an organization, we should have a clear idea of its mission as well as how the main parts of the organization work together to fulfill that mission. Starting with the organization's <u>clients</u>, we should know who they are and how we can best serve them. It is important to treat them with respect and listen to them so that we can better understand their needs. In my opinion, it is useful to have representatives of clients on the board of directors so that they will have a part in the decision-making process of the organization.

Who are the <u>donors</u> to the organization? These we should also treat with respect, honesty, and gratitude. Their funds are the life-blood of the organization, and they should not be subject to exaggerated appeals. Organizations need to give donors regular feedback on the use of their funds, and should respect any restrictions they make about their use.

<u>Board members and other volunteers</u> are other key players in an organization. They sacrificially give not only money, but time and thought to an organization. It is important that they have useful tasks, meaningful both to them and to the organization. Organizations should train them so that they understand well the mission and goals of the NGO as well as its operating philosophy. The board of a not-for-profit organization is usually the final authority of the organization and is responsible for hiring and firing the Chief Executive Officer.

The <u>Chief Executive Officer (CEO) and paid staff</u> of the organization are responsible for the day-to-day activities of the organization, from program activities to fundraising. The staff reports to the CEO, who in turn reports to the board of directors. The staff, board, and donors should be in harmony as to their understanding of the mission, strategy, and procedures of the organization. Mutual respect, coordination, and clear lines of communication between them are vital for success. Confusion and conflict often occur when individual board members bypass the rest of the board or the CEO to give directions to staff.

If the organization is to achieve its objectives, <u>other stake-holders</u> in the not-for-profit should also be consulted and their opinions considered. These stake-holders represent a wide variety of people and organizations including businesses that supply the organization, government, other partner agencies, regulatory agencies, funders, family members of clients, neighborhood organizations, etc.

As we noted before, organizations are like people. They cooperate with one another and they also compete. It is human nature that we should want "our" organizations to be the biggest, the richest, and the best. Competition can inspire better programs, but it can also lead to unwarranted pride and inefficiency. As much as possible, we should create a climate of cooperation between our organization and others in order to make our services stretch further. This cooperation can be in the guise of establishing mutually accepted guidelines and standards; sharing referrals, research data, and training opportunities; and pooling financial and staff resources for projects too big for only one organization. So much more good could be done if we did not worry so much about who gets credit for it. This is a truth we all know, but one that we rarely put into practice.

Often it is useful for not-for-profits to join in temporary coalitions or in formal federations in order to advance a mutual cause. This way they can share lobbying, program, or fundraising activities. We can see this sort of cooperation in community chambers of commerce, United Ways, and in federations of organizations interested in a particular cause. In my personal experience, the International Federation of Anti-Leprosy Organizations (ILEP) was a model of how not-for-profits can cooperate with each other, with governments, and with super-national organizations like the World Health Organization to reduce or eliminate a disease or solve a problem.

Raising money is a primary concern of almost all organizations, especially not-for-profits. It seems that they never have enough of it, and every year there is pressure to surpass the fundraising totals of the previous year. Increasingly, we hire and fire the presidents of NGOs, from great universities to community grass-root organizations, primarily on their ability to raise money.

While most fund-raising is ethical, sometimes fundraisers create emotional or truth-bending appeals that degrade or mislead people in the process. They justify themselves with the defense that it is the only way to get people to reach into their pockets. Sometimes the temptation they face is to raise money for a popular program, but to use it for a less popular one without the permission of the donor. Sometimes, it is to camouflage just how much of the donor's money is spent in fundraising and administration, rather than on the actual program for which they raised the money. Sometimes older people with poor memories and reasoning abilities are pressured to give beyond their means. Often, the vanity of the giver is appealed to and manipulated in order to get the resources the organization needs. All fundraisers and donors should be aware of these temptations and fight them.

## ADAPTING TO CHANGE

As we have said, in order for not-for-profit organizations to be effective, they have to have clear missions and strategies, blending the diverse interests of stakeholders. Most important, they also have to meet real needs in a community. If they do not, they will not survive for long. Therefore, not-for-profits must constantly be sensitive to changing discoveries, policies, and community needs, and be willing to adapt their missions and programs to these new situations. Sometimes not-for-profits are the catalysts for needed change, and sometimes they aggressively resist it because it is so difficult and painful to everyone involved. To illustrate the necessity and the difficulties of adapting to changing conditions, I will cite a personal example.

As I have said before, for many years of my professional life, I worked for the cure, rehabilitation, and social integration of people affected by leprosy, which in some countries is called Hansen's disease in order to reduce its stigma. When I began working with leprosy in the early 1970s, there were an estimated 12 to 15 million people with the disease in the world. These people were treated mostly in segregated hospitals and social institutions called leprosaria, or in segregated outpatient clinics only serving those with the disease. Health authorities, fearing contagion, often separated the young healthy children of people with the disease into special orphanages. Governments and leprosy fundraising organizations, usually religious in nature and based in countries with few leprosy cases, supported with their finances this segregated system of treatment. The stigma of leprosy was intense, and people often hid their disease and even changed their family names because of it.

Today, things have changed dramatically. Instead of 12 to 15 million people, there are now less than a million people with Hansen's disease in the world. This remarkable reduction in numbers was achieved by the discovery of an effective cure for the disease and by the close cooperation of the World Health Organization, national governments, and not-for-profit organizations in a campaign to get the cure to as many people as quickly as possible.

Parallel to the discovery of a cure for the disease, other scientific findings also played an important part in changing the way we treat people with the disease. These included the finding that not all types of Hansen's disease are contagious, and that people in treatment for even the contagious types of the disease, are actually very low risks to others as the vast majority of people have a natural resistance to the disease. Furthermore, researchers determined that most of the deformities and disabilities, once associated with the disease, could be prevented. All of these discoveries together helped reduce the fear of leprosy and caused many to question the usefulness and morality of continuing to maintain an expensive, unnecessary, and stigmatizing structure of segregated institutions to treat a decreasing number of people with the disease.

Those of us who opted for radically transforming the system have been largely successful, and today, most of the segregated institutions that were once the backbone for leprosy work, have been dismantled or integrated and now treat not only people with Hansen's disease, but also persons with other medical or social problems unrelated to the disease.

During this time of new discoveries and institutional change, many people affected by Hansen's disease also began to organize and demand more participation in the medical and socio-economic decisions and in the organizations that affected their lives. They wanted their voices and opinions to be heard. Some of them fought against integration because they feared losing the security and the medical, economic, and social support they had come to expect in leprosaria. Others, who lived integrated in society, spoke out forcefully against the terribly negative image of the disease sometimes spread by preachers, fundraisers, and the media. These images, they felt, were demeaning and inaccurate and made it harder for them to lead normal lives.

Leprosy work has thus been revolutionized for the good over the last four or five decades, but the transformation process has been painful for just about everyone involved in it. For example, <u>operators of leprosaria</u> and other segregated leprosy institutions saw their client numbers decrease, and they had to come to a difficult decision to either close or to remake their institutions in relevant and economically viable ways. Many resisted change at first, but finally the dwindling numbers of people with the disease and the high financial cost and stigmatizing impact of leprosy-only organizations and institutions could no longer be ignored. They had to integrate and expand their services to others or close for lack of clients and funds.

<u>Leprologists</u> or leprosy medical specialists also saw their influence and prestige diminish as patient numbers dropped and leprosy institutions began to treat other medical problems besides Hansen's disease. They, too, had to learn how to adapt and to practice new skills in wider and more competitive medical worlds.

<u>Leprosy fundraising organizations</u> had to face many strategic and ethical issues as well as most patients began to be treated in integrated, government-sponsored programs and not in their own not-for-profit leprosy institutions. Should these fundraising organizations continue to focus just on leprosy as their early founders wished, or should they expand their missions to include other problems like AIDs, tuberculosis, disability, or other dermatological problems to reflect the new reality in the field of fewer patients and integrated treatment? What should they do about their highly successful fundraising appeals? Ethically, it was hard to continue to imply to potential donors that any donated funds would go to curing children with leprosy in Christian leprosy programs when the new reality was that, by far, most of their money was now going to treating the medical and social problems of adults in government programs that also served non-leprosy patients. Changing fundraising messages was difficult for some organizations because they were well aware of the power of leprosy, of stigma, of religion, and of children in raising money.

<u>People affected by the disease</u> also had to face their own difficult questions in this period of transformation. While everyone applauded

whole-heartedly the new cure and disability prevention programs, some institutionalized persons who long had complained of their having been forced into leprosaria in the past, now saw themselves as being forced out into the community as these institutions closed or became integrated. Naturally, they did not like it. Some of those who had special pensions because of their leprosy now feared losing these pensions, as leprosy became "a disease like any other." Some who knew that their disease should carry no shame, still struggled to "come out of the closet" because they also knew that they and their family might still be stigmatized.

Those persons, who were <u>catalysts</u> for integration and structural and attitudinal change in the leprosy world, also struggled and suffered. Many of those holding to the traditional segregated ways of treating people with the disease perceived them and their efforts as being too radical and strongly resisted them. Those in the non-leprosy world also often opposed them as they had their own fears and prejudices about welcoming people affected by leprosy into their own medical, disability, or socio-economic programs. Even many disabled person organizations, that should have known better, did not wish to include in their ranks those disabled by leprosy.

## SOME LESSONS LEARNED

At least three important lessons about the challenges facing not-for-profits can be extracted from this experience in the world of Hansen's disease:

*A first lesson is that the solutions of the past may become the impediments of the present.* When organizations like leprosaria and orphanages for the healthy children of people affected by leprosy were founded many years ago by brave and generous men and women, they were good and proper solutions for some very serious problems at that time. However, as knowledge increased about the disease and a cure for it became available, these past solutions became unnecessary, expensive, and stigmatizing obstacles. Organizations have to adapt to changing times and information if they are to survive and be effective. Changing knowledge must lead to changing structures even though such change is sometimes very painful as it goes against entrenched interests.

*A second lesson is that "the medium is the message."* How not-for-profits raise funds and how they deliver their services to their clients play a strong role in shaping the public's opinion about their cause. Stigmatizing service delivery systems and fundraising techniques can have a very negative effect on the lives of the people targeted for assistance. In the case of Hansen's disease, continuing to treat people in segregated programs and institutions and continuing to raise money by emphasizing only the religious history of leprosy makes it much harder to get rid of the leprosy stigma and of society's fear of the disease and to help people affected by the disease to lead normal lives. If our fundraising tactics presents those we are trying to help in too pitiful and emotional a way, it will be hard for the public to treat them with the dignity and opportunities that they deserve.

*Third, recipients of services should always have some part in the design of programs for their benefit.* The input of clients who receive help is just as valuable as that of the donors who give money, and that of the professionals who deliver services. Each perspective is important. In the early 1980's, I was amazed to witness in one international conference on Hansen's disease that the majority of the professional participants in the congress voted against inviting representatives of people affected by the disease to the next conference to share their experiences and suggestions for improving care. Thankfully, that would not happen today.

In summary, not-for-profit organizations are wonderful tools for doing much good in the world. They have freedom of action that governments do not have, and so they can quickly adjust to changing needs and events. However, not-for-profit organizations can also do a lot of unintentional harm if, in the interest of gaining influence and resources, the truth is fudged, the people they are to help are exploited, and programs are designed without the input of all of the organization's stakeholders. Sometimes we need to look at our organizations just as we need to look at ourselves. We need to be thankful for our successes, but we also need to understand and to correct our failures. After all, our organizations were formed to do good, and we want them to be and do the best that they can.

Now that we have looked at how we can do good individually as well as with others in governments and NGOs, let us turn our attention to the next part of this book—the problems we face as we try to apply what we have learned to other nations and peoples. How can we do our part "to make the world a better place"?

# PART III
## MAKING THE WORLD A BETTER PLACE

*"Go ye into all the world . . ."*

*(Matthew 28:19)*

# CHAPTER 14
## INTERNATIONAL NEIGHBORS

Today, more than at any other time in history, we live in an international community. Instantaneous communication through the internet and satellite television, as well as relatively inexpensive air transportation, have made us acutely aware of peoples and cultures with which we used to have little or no contact.

We are all connected in other ways as well. The exhaust from the cars of North America, the factories of China, and the cows of India affect our globe's ozone level. The products that we buy in stores in the U.S.A. are made with iron ore from South America, labor from Asia, and design from Europe. One now goes to a local Wal-Mart, even in rural towns in the U.S.A., and sees people whose roots are from all over the world. The world is changing and shrinking.

With this instantaneous communication and inter-dependence, the definition of who is our neighbor has expanded to include the whole world. Whether out of compassion, guilt, fear, or self-interest, we in the rich parts of the world now look at those in poorer regions and ask ourselves what we should do to help? How should we as individuals, NGOs, and governments act to create a better world in which we can all live in prosperity and at peace with one another?

To begin to answer that question, I find it helpful to first look at our own personal attitudes about foreign assistance, as our attitudes will color greatly our goals and strategies for reaching out to the people of other nations. Specifically, what are our beliefs about nations, cultures, and races that are different from our own; about international law; and about wealth and sharing? Let us look at each of these separately.

***Our view of "foreigners."*** Do we think of people of other nations as competitors or collaborators, as enemies or as brothers and sisters of the same Father? In our view, does God love Americans more than the Chinese, Europeans more than Africans, Israelis more than Iranians, the rich more than the poor, or vice versa? In our view, are certain races or nationalities inferior or superior to others?

The more we view others as people like ourselves with similar worth and aspirations, the more we will see them as potential friends and want to help them. It is not so hard to share some of one's wealth with people whom one considers as friends.

***Our view of interference in the affairs of other nations.*** One part of us balks at a call for involvement in the affairs and problems of other nations and of their citizens. We have enough problems in our own families and countries, and it is pretentious to think that we have the wisdom or the resources to solve the problems of others. Besides, people of other nations resent our interference in their affairs just as we resent their interference in our own.

Another part of us tells us, however, that we should be involved. We are our brother's keeper and they are ours. How we relate nation to nation is similar to the way we relate to others as individuals. We all need each other. We need friendly nations that will not attack us, that will supply our needs in raw materials and products, and that in return will buy our products and services. We need the companies of other nations that will work with our own companies to produce cars, planes, TVs, and many other multinational products. Our mutual funds invest in these foreign companies and we benefit financially from their success. We need other countries to buy our bonds and to help maintain the stability of our money and our life styles. We need other nations to cooperate with us to stop the spread of pollution, diseases, and criminal behavior that do not respect national boundaries. We need to coordinate with them to deal with natural disasters that affect us all. We need to pay them fairly for what they sell us so that they will have money to create jobs, purchase our products and services, and retain their citizens. Making sure that other countries are stable, safe, and prosperous helps curtail illegal immigration to our own nation, makes them desirable locations to do business, and makes them inviting destinations to visit as tourists. In so many ways, our national success is tied to the success of other nations.

***Our view of right and wrong.*** Our views of justice and injustice also help determine how willing we are to help or to interfere in the life of other nations.

First, do we believe that there are universal standards of right and wrong imbedded in all people by their Creator, or do we believe that right and wrong are concepts that are totally relative to cultures? Do we believe that universal human rights trump national sovereignty, or are they subordinate to it?

Second, do we believe in reciprocity and equal standards for all nations, or do we believe that some nations should be held to different standards? The world is full of examples of differing standards being applied for "our" nation as opposed to the standards we apply for "their" nation—from nuclear power to religious freedom. A particularly thorny issue, in which nations are especially inconsistent, is in their claims to territory. For example, who now has the right to the land of Palestine? Should it be the Israelis, who have lived there for the past 50 years, or should it be the Palestinians and their children who were expelled 50 years earlier? If the Jews should give up their territory to the Muslims whom they conquered, should the Muslims then give back to the Christians the lands that they conquered from them? Should the U.S.A. give its western lands back to Mexico, which it defeated, then Mexico give those lands to the Indians?

Third, what is our view of the use of power? Is it right for one nation to use military, economic, or political pressure on another to get its way? When, if ever, is it right for nations to invade other nations militarily? Should there be a world justice system that would make binding decisions involving disagreements between nations, and a world police force to carry out those decisions?

We all know that no nation or individual is totally consistent or logical in its views on these and many other matters. We have all been conquerors and conquered, have spied and been spied upon, have discriminated against and been given special privileges. For that reason, the only way to have peace is to work from the point of view that each of the opposing sides in a dispute has some of the truth on their side, and that the only way to solve matters is to compromise in a fair and loving way.

***Our view of wealth and poverty.*** Our philosophical and emotional positions about wealth and poverty also have a tremendous effect on how we think about helping the people of other nations. When I was a college student studying and hitchhiking in France, I was picked up once by the head of the Communist Party in Marseille who was driving a very expensive sports car. In our ensuing conversation he defended himself saying that he saw no incongruence in his expressed concern for the poor laborer and in his owning such an expensive car. His objective, he said, was to bring the poor laborer up to his level rather than for him to go down to the laborer's economic level.

In other words, his view of wealth was that it was abundant and not limited. He did not have give up his own wealth in order to help someone else to be prosperous. When we feel that wealth is limited, then we resist sharing what we have with others. Their gain would be our loss. However, if we believe that wealth is abundant and that in sharing our talents, technology, and riches with others, we can both keep what we have and maybe even gain something, then we are much more likely to help others. No doubt, some types of wealth are limited, but it is also true that many types of wealth can be multiplied through ingenuity, inventions, discoveries, hard work, and trade so that both the investor and those invested in prosper. Helping others can be a win-win situation.

Another view of wealth that affects our generosity to others is our view of the connection between wealth and merit. Do we believe that wealth is mostly a reward for hard work, or mostly due to good fortune? Are people wealthy mostly because of their ingenuity, or mostly because of their having been born into a privileged sex, class, race, family, and nation?

What do we think about the opposite? Is poverty one's own fault—the result of inferior character and laziness? Or is it mainly the result of bad luck, unfair institutional systems and structures that condemn a people to fewer opportunities for education, nutrition, medical services, and capital? If we see poverty as one's own fault, then of course we will be less empathetic to the poor.

When do we have enough wealth? The answer we give to that question also makes a difference in our level of generosity. It is hard to know when we have enough wealth. Most of us conclude that we do not have enough, especially now that life spans are longer and medical costs are astronomical. We fear becoming a burden to others. The reality is that we are only truly wealthy when we are content with what we have, and trust in God for our future.

Finally, do we consider ourselves the legitimate owners of our wealth or only stewards while we are alive on this earth? If we feel responsible to a higher benevolent Authority as to how we use our money, then we will tend to be more generous.

In summary, the more that we are content with what we have, see wealth as abundant and not limited, see ourselves as stewards and not owners of our wealth, and do not totally blame others for their poverty, then the more likely we are to be generous to others, including those of other countries.

Once we are aware of our own attitudes towards helping people of other nations and aware of our inclinations towards one country or another, we can then turn our attention to how we should best help them. What should be our goals as individuals, government, and NGOs in helping those in other countries? What kind of societies do we want to live in ourselves and help create abroad?

# IN WHAT KIND OF SOCIETIES DO WE WANT TO LIVE?

From what I gather from my experience in different countries, almost all persons want to live in societies that are:

*Secure:* We all want to be and feel safe from outside threats of invasion and from inside threats of physical violence and loss of property. We want to be safe as much as we can from human error and human meanness and from disastrous natural events.

*Prosperous:* We all want to lead the "good life" in material terms. That means having access to food, clean air and water, health resources, clothing, a comfortable home, a good education, opportunities for recreation, an interesting job, and an agreeable environment.

*Free:* We all want to have the freedom to believe what we believe, to say what we believe, to marry whom we want to marry, to raise our children in the way we feel is correct, to associate with whom we want, to work and live where we feel is best. We do not want to live in an overly regulated society that hampers us unnecessarily.

*Just:* We all want to live in a society where the rules are logical, fair, and consistent (at least for us!). We want a society where those who break the rules are treated in a way that restrains them, but where the punishment is humane, fits the crime, and involves reforming the law-breaker.

*Respected:* We all want to feel good about ourselves both as individuals and as citizens of our nations. We want to have a life of meaning and purpose and have others see us, see our society, and see our nation in a positive light.

*Hopeful:* We all want to believe that in the future things will get better for us, for our children, and for other loved ones.

While we all yearn for similar blessings, some societies do better than others in providing them to their citizens. Some succeed and some fail. Why is this so? Let us look at some of the possible reasons:

# WHY DO SOME SOCIETIES SUCCEED AND OTHERS FAIL?

No society is perfect, but some nations or societies fail more than others do economically, socially, and politically. Their failures can lead to short and difficult lives for their citizens, to mass emigration, and to violent revolutions. Some of the most common reasons for such societal failures seem to be the following:

*Lack of useful natural resources:* There are countries that have been blessed with abundant natural resources and others that have few. Large reserves of metal ores, precious stones, coal, oil, gas, forests, agricultural land, and fishing zones are all important to a nation's wealth and standard of living. Some nations have rivers that can generate electricity and facilitate travel and commerce while others do not. Some also have natural beauty which attracts tourists and therefore income for the nation, while others lack this asset. Those nations with long coastlines and natural harbors have much greater possibilities for trade than mountainous landlocked countries.

*Human resource problems:* These natural resources, however, must be utilized in some way to generate wealth. There is thus a need for capable, educated citizens. And if a country has few natural resources, then it becomes even more important to have competent and skilled citizens who are young and healthy to do the invention, the business deals, the manufacturing, the farming, and other activities that also generate wealth. Population size is also an issue. Too small a population means not enough people to do the work, and too large a population means a division of national wealth in more ways, leaving less for each person.

*Infrastructure problems:* Infrastructure including electrical generating plants and grids, roads, railroads, shipping, harbors, telecommunications, water and sewage lines, health centers, hospitals, public health programs, schools, and universities are all essential for creating and maintaining an educated and healthy population and for allowing that population to create and exchange wealth. Poor countries usually have precarious infrastructures.

**Large debt:** Nations that have large internal or external debt are hampered in their ability to produce wealth, as they must continually be paying off both interest and principal. Taking out loans can be a good path to development, if the money received goes to purchasing the materials, equipment, and infrastructures that lead to the production of wealth. On the other hand, loans can devastate a country if they are diverted to non-productive projects, or wasted by corruption.

**Unfavorable climate and location:** Climate is another factor that influences a nation's wealth. While hot tropical climates can produce abundant food, they can also foster parasites and diseases that decimate populations and rob survivors of energy and initiative. Colder climates force people to plan, work hard, and save, as they know that their window of opportunity for growing and gathering is limited. In addition, climate and location have a big impact on natural disasters like hurricanes, tornadoes, earthquakes, and floods. In a moment, these can wreck the economic potential of a nation and the lives of its citizens.

**History:** Each country has its own history, and these histories influence what a people think about themselves and others. Some countries have had their national boundaries drawn by outsiders who did not take into account ethnic, tribal, and religious loyalties. Some countries see themselves as historical victims of other countries and therefore may have a lower sense of self-esteem, initiative, and desire to cooperate with others. Some countries carry heavy burdens of shame from their past actions with regard to minorities within their own borders or in their treatment of other countries.

**Politics and culture:** The politics and culture of a country also have a big role to play in a country's prosperity. Countries that place high priority in the health and education of all their citizens, including women and minorities, do better than those that do not. Democratic countries, with transparent legal and financial systems, do better than countries with unfair legal systems that tolerate corruption and special privileges. Countries whose governments or major religious and political parties are repressive do not do as well as countries that are not.

***Lack of good leadership:*** Some nations are led by ineffective or greedy leaders who place their own power and wealth and that of their family and cronies before that of their people. Others have good leaders who lay the foundations for future prosperity.

***Lack of international cooperation:*** All nations need each other. Some nations have done poorly because they have isolated themselves from international partnerships, while others have prospered, in part because of these partnerships.

Nation building, or dealing with some of the above problems, is a primary objective of the international aid of many governments and super-national organizations such as the U.N. They hope to transform societies at a macro level.

We, of course, as individuals and as NGOs have much more modest goals. Our focus is primarily on individuals of other countries and on the small communities in which they live. It is our hope that by our support we can transform the lives of people and their communities and that they then will go on to transform their societies. Just as we looked at some of the reasons that some nations are successful and others are not, let us now consider some of the probable reasons for the economic success or failure of individuals within those countries.

## WHY DO SOME INDIVIDUALS SUCCEED ECONOMICALLY AND OTHERS FAIL?

Why do some persons fail and others succeed? Within successful countries, some people fail, and within countries that are failures, some people succeed. What factors are important for individual economic success? Here are a few that I have found to be important:

***Desire and hope for a better life:*** The starting point for any successful change is the recognition by a person of the need to change followed by the desire for something different and better. Desire is a motor that impels people through an obstacle-strewn path towards

125

success. Desire for a better life makes us work harder to get the money we require to pay for the education that will help lift our children out of poverty or to purchase the house that will give our family more comfort and security. Desire incites us to think creatively and discover new products and services that others might want or need and for which they would be willing to pay.

**Good character traits:** Self-discipline and a sense of individual responsibility are two character traits important to individual economic and social success. In the process of training and placing disabled persons in jobs in Brazil, we found that employers wanted reliable and responsible workers who showed up on time, worked steadily, took good care of their tools, helped their co-workers, and did not use their physical condition as an excuse. Other more company-oriented skills they could learn on the job. People who succeed in bettering their lives are proactive. They take the initiative and do not wait for the government, an international NGO, or lottery winnings to save them. People who succeed over the long run are also people who play by the rules and are fair, cooperative, and respectful of others. They live within their means, foregoing immediate gratification for long-term goals.

**Physical and mental health:** Physical and mental health are also basic to economic progress. That is why it is so important for governments to invest in a good primary healthcare system with emphasis on the prevention of problems. In developing countries, preventable diseases such as AIDS, malaria, and tuberculosis decimate the work force and keep families and countries mired in poverty. Simple inexpensive solutions from vaccines to mosquito nets, clean water sources, abstinence, condoms, and health education can turn the tide in many cases.

**Education:** Education is extremely important to the success of individuals. Education teaches us how to reason, how to get information, as well as how to be creative. Going to school daily teaches us self-discipline, goal attainment, and social skills. Education stirs our vision of a better life and a better world for ourselves and for others. It gives us the technical skills that we need to succeed, and the tolerance that we need to get along.

***Capital:*** Whatever the business one decides to begin, from the smallest sidewalk vendor to the largest industry, there must be initial capital to set up shop, to buy initial supplies and equipment. This money has to come from somewhere. It can come from money that one has saved, or from a gift of a relative. It can come in the form of investment by someone who believes in the potential of one's business, or it may come in the form of a loan from an individual, a bank, or a development agency.

People give loans to people because they feel that the loan recipients are trustworthy. The expectation is that they will fulfill their promise to repay the loan with interest. Still, lenders normally require that collateral be put-up as a guarantee of payment in case there is a default. One of the big problems in development is that poor people have little or no property that they can put up as collateral. Nor do they have friends who can co-sign notes for them. Another problem they face is that interest rates for small and risky loans are quite high and eat up much of the profit of a small new enterprise. Many development agencies have experimented with creative new ways for dealing with these problems and have thus contributed to bettering the lives of millions of formerly impoverished people.

***Opportunities and support systems:*** Of course, some people are fortunate to have support systems and opportunities that others do not have. These have to do with where they live, who their parents are, their physical and intellectual abilities, and the availability of educational and employment opportunities for them. They also have to do with access to new inventions that save labor and facilitate communication and with new discoveries and techniques that increase food supplies and energy. They also consist of people taking an interest in them, opening doors for them, giving them ideas and material support. Our task in international development is to help provide these opportunities for those we target.

# How can we help internationally?

This leads us to how we can help individuals and nations other than our own overcome some of their problems and reach their highest potentials. We don't even have to leave our own country to do so. We can start by helping the "foreigners" living within our own country.

Here at home, we have millions of international strangers in our midst—people who have come to our country as students, visitors, or as immigrants. We can help them to adapt to our culture and to feel welcomed. We can invite them into our homes and churches, teach them English, give them jobs, help them with legal requirements. We can give time and money to local organizations that sponsor relief and development efforts and that promote the respect for human rights around the world. We can support community events to promote understanding between cultures. We can buy and sell the products of the nations that we feel called to help. We can lobby our government and our non-governmental agencies to take an interest in specific causes and nations and to give more foreign assistance. We can learn of the special needs of people of other nationalities and pray for them.

Overseas, we can visit other countries as tourists, as businesspersons, as volunteer helpers. We can seek employment in government and non-governmental agencies that are involved in providing foreign assistance to the countries to which we are particularly attracted.

Foreign assistance is often categorized into three main areas: emergency assistance, reconstruction assistance, and development assistance. In <u>emergency assistance,</u> the goal is to provide the basics for survival to vulnerable people who are victims of war, natural disasters, epidemics, and famines. Such basics include food, water, clothing, shelter, medical care, and security. The underlying philosophy of emergency assistance is to get help as quickly as we can to people who are in trouble. This help is usually short-term, paternalistic in nature, and administered from the top down. <u>Reconstruction assistance</u> is given in the immediate phase after emergency assistance and its main goal is to replace the infrastructure that was destroyed by the disaster. It usually lasts longer than emergency assistance. <u>Development assistance</u> has much more ambitious goals than either emergency or reconstruction assistance. Its main objective is to help a region become safe, prosperous, and self-sufficient. Development assistance takes much longer and has goals that are harder to achieve than the other two, but if successful, it can transform a recipient of aid into a giver of aid.

As we contemplate the best way to help a poor region or group of people develop, we must make many decisions. One decision is about where we should concentrate our intervention in order to have the most "bang for the buck." For example, should we focus on the prevention of problems or on reacting to those that already exist? Is it best to concentrate on security, or on health, education, and culture? Should we give the bulk of our assistance to special groups like women, children, minorities, or to those living in a limited geographical area, or should we try to help the general population? Should our assistance be money, goods, equipment, buildings, technical assistance, or all of the above? Should we give our aid to government, to non-governmental institutions, or directly to individuals? Should we, the donors, determine how the aid will be used, or should we let those receiving the aid determine how they will use it? If we set conditions, what sort of conditions should we set? What sort of accountability processes should we put into place? Should we give our aid directly or should we pool our aid with others in order to have a bigger impact? Should our aid be in the form of outright gifts, in the forms of loans that are to be re-paid, or in the form of investments and partnerships?

Recipients of international aid often complain about the conditions that donors attach to such aid. One major complaint is that the money provided comes in the form of loans with high interest rates instead of as outright gifts or investments. Recipients of aid also complain about what they consider are other self-serving conditions that donor nations sometimes place on gifts or loans—such as insisting that the money be used to buy products or technical assistance from the donor nation, or that any transportation of products and materials be done only in the ships and planes of the donor nation. They also do not like that so much of the aid money goes not to their own nationals but to expatriate technical advisors, providing for their comparatively high salaries, housing, and vehicle costs. They would prefer it go to local people and companies. At other times, recipients of aid object to what they consider the donor's air of superiority and interference in their own internal affairs, attaching what the recipients consider unacceptable conditions to their giving of aid.

Giving organizations, on the other hand, have their own concerns and complaints about recipient nations and institutions. Donors, of course, want their resources to be used for the purposes for which they were intended and so are justifiably concerned about corruption, the lack of transparency, and the diversion of funds and equipment from agreed upon purposes. They are also troubled about inefficiency in the use of the donated money or supplies, such as when donated food sits rotting in warehouses instead of getting to the people who need it. Since donors sometimes want to use their gifts as leverage to promote human rights or political positions more in line with their own, they are upset when recipients of aid do not follow through on agreed upon reforms.

The bottom line is that we need much wisdom in giving assistance at the international level. As mentioned earlier, a major danger in any kind of assistance is that in trying to solve one problem, we create other more serious ones. As we know, if we give out welfare checks to the poor, we can sometimes foster low self-esteem and unnecessary dependence. If we give subsidies to farms and businesses, we can help turn them into inefficient and non-competitive organizations. If we separate people by interning them in institutions, we run the risk of making them institutionalized and dependent. If we provide free or low priced food for too long, we run the risk of putting local farmers out of business. If we enter a country with a military force for a short-term engagement, we may find ourselves stuck in an undesirable long-range commitment. If we give too much aid to a country for too long, they may become unnecessarily reliant on that aid.

Trying to do good to our international neighbors and make the world a better place is thus a complicated and difficult undertaking that requires a good heart and a good head. Sometimes development works, and nations and individuals are lifted out of poverty and become largely self-sufficient. Sometimes it does not, and they remain stuck in poverty and forever dependent. Examples can be given of both types of experiences in all parts of the world. Although our efforts to help other nations and their people often fail, we should not give up trying. Instead, we should learn from our mistakes and modify our programs accordingly. We are always getting a little better at it.

# CHAPTER 15
## *LIVING AND WORKING IN ANOTHER CULTURE*

One satisfying way to help people of other nations is to devote some of our vacation time to short-term assistance projects overseas. Work-project tourism is a major activity by foreigners in many developing countries. Some volunteer work-projects are secular or political in nature, such as the work brigades organized to help the Sandinistas bring in coffee crops during Nicaragua's civil war in the 1980s. Most others, however, are sponsored by religious groups and usually consist of teams put together to evangelize, to provide medical treatment, to dig wells, to construct houses, churches, and schools, or to offer technical advice.

Some question the efficiency of such short-term projects as they take a lot of time to plan and coordinate. They can also end up costing a lot more than hiring locals to do the same task if one considers the costs of airfares, housing, and other volunteer expenses. For that reason, many argue that it is much better to send money to a project rather than to go as a volunteer. Besides, the locals need the jobs.

While admitting to these drawbacks, defenders of work-project tourism argue that the advantages of such projects outweigh the disadvantages. The trips give service opportunities to the volunteers; they foster friendships and mutual respect between people of different nationalities and cultures; they also bring new money into the country. When the volunteer returns to his or her home country, he or she usually serves as an ambassador of good will and in the process generates more interest, tourism, and perhaps resources for other projects in the country.

While some people find it hard to get away for longer than a week or two to visit another country, others want to devote much more time to living abroad as students, retirees, aid workers, missionaries, Peace Corps volunteers, teachers, diplomats, and businesspersons. Living in a different land and culture from one's own carries with it a number of challenges, however. Two of these are learning a new language and a new way of looking at the world. A third is deciding how much we should adapt to this new way of seeing the world and when we should act according to our own culture and beliefs. When should we go native and live, dress, and act like the locals, and when should we hang out with those of our own nationality and stick with our own ways of doing things?

Some missionaries, businesspersons, and other foreigners come into a country and continue to live as if they had never left their homeland. Sometimes they even try to impose their own way of dress, architecture, moral codes, political systems, and language on others. In fact, in this age of western cultural domination, much of the world is beginning to look and act the same. Stores, restaurants, and airports around the world all have similar appearances and businesspersons from many nations crisscross the world each day wearing the same type of clothing and increasingly speaking the same language of English. Still, many local ways of doing things differ markedly from our own. Since being good and doing good involves respecting the sensibilities of others, it might be useful at this point to review some of them.

## CULTURAL CHALLENGES TO LIVING IN ANOTHER COUNTRY

*Laws:* Laws differ from country to country, and we should be aware of these differences and respect them. Some cultures also see laws more as guidelines rather than as standards to obey at all times. As a personal example, in one country where I once lived, the law said that citizens and visitors should exchange foreign money only in official banks. So, for many years, that is what I did, even though my friends and co-workers constantly made fun of me. They told me that I was a fool for doing so as the parallel exchange rate "on the street," was often as much as 75% higher than the official exchange rate that I was getting. They themselves thought nothing of "breaking the law" as everyone did it and newspapers and television daily posted both the official and the unofficial rates of the day. Finally, after years of losing very significant amounts of personal money and aid funds by exchanging my dollars in the bank, I decided to speak about the matter with a top official in the country's central bank with whom I was having a meeting on another subject. I told him that while I wanted to obey the law, I also did not want to be a fool. After hearing me out, this high official looked at me from where he was sitting behind his desk and said, "The law should be obeyed." Then he got up from his chair, walked around it to the front of the desk, and said to me unofficially, "But in your case, you should change your money on the parallel market."

***Tips and bribes:*** Similarly, countries have different views about what is an appropriate incentive or financial tip for doing a good job, and what is an illegal bribe. In some countries, police and other government workers often depend on "contributions" to supplement low salaries, much as waiters in other countries depend on tips. These small gifts are extended for services like hurrying up paperwork, allowing for a warning instead of a fine, or bending the law in some other way. Persons, from other cultures, struggle with whether to "tip" the police officer who just pulled them over for a minor traffic violation or whether to report him to his supervisors for corruption when he asks for "a little money to help buy gas for our vehicles." Many times, in order to avoid hassle and to get what one wants, the small tip-bribe seems the easiest option.

***Special consideration:*** Even without tips or bribes, in some cultures, one expects government workers to extend special favors to friends. In other cultures, one sees such special treatment as unfair and so it is unlawful.

***Politeness and respect for authority:*** Likewise, certain people and positions carry immense respect and authority in some cultures, and one treats them in a deferential way. In other countries, people take delight in treating everyone with frankness and as equals.

*Gratitude:* People express gratitude differently in different cultures. Sometimes it is effusive, and at other times, very understated so as not to embarrass either the giver or the recipient.

*Personal space and privacy:* Customs around the world also differ regarding personal space and privacy. For example, in some countries, people speak right in your face, and in others, that would be threatening and rude. In some places, men walk down the streets holding hands with each other out of friendship. In other cultures, people might see this as showing sexual preference. In some cultures, people would most likely be offended if a stranger asked them about how much they earned, while in other cultures, they would not. Some cultures stress personal cleanliness more than others. Some stress frankness, and others are much more oblique and polite. Some feel that smoking and loud music in public places is an affront, while others hardly notice people smoking or personal radios blaring on beaches and buses.

*Relationships between the sexes:* Some cultures strictly restrain the mixing of the sexes, while others are much more open and lenient. Some allow public display of affection between the sexes that other cultures would consider scandalous. Some cultures strictly limit educational and job opportunities for women, while others consider such limitations a violation of human rights. Dress also differs from society to society and some cultures are much more conservative as to the public display of the body.

*Body language and the meaning of words:* Similar words can take on different meaning in different cultures, and the same body language can signify entirely different intentions.

*Environment:* How we treat the environment also differs from culture to culture. Some cultures see little harm in throwing trash out of cars on to highways and contaminating rivers and air. Others are highly conscious of the environment and the need for its protection.

*Food and drink:* Some cultures are mainly vegetarian. Others eat meat, but are highly selective as to what types of meat are permissible. Some ban pork, and others are horrified if one eats dogs, horses, rodents, and insects. Some cultures find nothing wrong with drinking alcohol in moderation, while others totally forbid its consumption.

*Time:* The importance of time differs from culture to culture and is often the source of many frustrations. Many expatriates, including myself, are literalists in terms of time and law, and people from many other cultures are not. We expect to arrive at meetings at times previously agreed upon with little error. To us, punctuality is a courtesy to all concerned and a necessity of efficiency. People of another culture are not nearly so strict and see such rigid punctuality as unnecessary and sometimes ungracious. In their view, the person one is with takes precedent over the person with whom one has an appointment.

*Religion:* Religion is also an area where customs and laws vary greatly. In some countries, church and state are separated strictly, and in others, there is little or no such separation. There is also very limited religious freedom. How and where one prays, what one is permitted to say and do, when one eats and what one eats, whom one marries, and how one dresses is regulated by religion in many countries.

*Beauty:* Concepts of beauty differ from person to person and culture to culture. We all have different concepts of what body types, hairstyles, makeup, clothes, music, and art we favor. We also have different ideas as to housing and to decorations. One person's gaudy is another person's lovely.

*Cultural superiority:* It is hard for rich persons from more-developed countries not to have superior attitudes to people in poorer countries. After all, we are the aid givers and not the aid recipients. However, it behooves us not to be so haughty. Many of those who are willing to accept our technical or financial help do not want to adopt our customs because they often see our ways as immoral, superficial, materialistic, and inferior to their own. Money and technical superiority are not everything!

Dealing with cultural conflicts in a foreign country is a daily occurrence for sensitive foreigners. We want to please and not offend, but we also want to be true to ourselves. So what do we do? Should we stick with our own ways of doing things, or should we adapt to the ways of the culture in which we are living?

After struggling with such questions for many years, I have come up with my own personal solution to the problem. I find it useful to think of myself as having three imaginary zones around me. The innermost zone defines who I am. The second zone is farther out and encloses my comfort levels, opinions, customs, and habits, but not my basic principles. Outside this second zone is a much larger third zone that encompasses things that I am neutral to or about which I have no strong opinion.

In this analogy, it is wrong for me to violate the basic principles of the innermost zone of who I am. On the other hand, while it might be painful, it would not be wrong for me to compromise on issues in the middle zone involving culture, comfort, opinions, and habits. And of course, I can and should easily adapt to anything in the outermost zone in order to fit into the new culture in which I am now living.

For example, if I am encouraged by people with other cultural views to accept what I consider lying, bribery, stealing, the exploitation of women or children, or to convert to a religion other than the one I believe in, then I must refuse. It would be wrong to adapt to that culture because that would mean sacrificing my basic beliefs and principles. If, on the other hand, they ask me to eat strange foods, wear different style clothes, modify my concepts of time and manners, then that I could maybe do. I would not necessarily like it, but I would be willing to do it if it would make a positive difference to my friends in the other culture. A safe guideline to follow is one St. Paul promulgates. We should hold on to the essentials that we consider good and true, but be willing to adapt in the non-essentials out of respect to others.

As for the questions of bribery and money exchange, I have come up with the following solution for myself: If I decide that I need to hide an action, then I try not to do it. If I can do the action openly or am willing to take the consequences for doing it, then the action is all right for me to do. I will not give what I consider bribes, but I will exchange money on the parallel market.

# CHOOSING A LIFE STYLE IN A POOR COUNTRY

We foreigners stick out in many countries because of our race, our dress, and our accents. Sometimes we like that because we get special privileges because of who we are. At other times, we do not like it, because it means that people are constantly pestering us. Sometimes it is for money, because they think we are wealthy; sometimes it is because they are berating us for something that our government is doing or has done. In such cases, we want to fit in and be ourselves, and not some representative of a particular race or nation.

Choosing an appropriate life style in another country much poorer than our own is another dilemma that raises concerns of conscience among many expatriates. Generally, expatriates who live in developing countries earn much more and have many more benefits than locals who have similar education levels and do similar work. We have nice houses, servants, fancy four-wheeled-drive vehicles, and private schools for our children well beyond what our local co-workers can afford, and completely beyond the means of the general population. Often we live in protected compounds that set us apart even more.

Those of us with sensitive consciences question if this is just. We wonder if we should live among those we have come to serve and be at a similar economic level. We ask ourselves if we foreigners are taking the jobs of locals, and if our much larger salaries and benefits are justified. Should their salaries be raised to our level or should our salaries be lowered to theirs?

While these questions eat at our consciences, we also find good reasons to justify our separate and elitist situation. We argue in our defense that those special compounds we live in may be necessary for security reasons. As for our houses, cars, and schools, we contend that our families should not have to suffer a lower living standard and our children an inferior education to what they would receive in our home nation just because we have chosen to work in a developing country. We are also helping the local economy with our purchases. When we hire maids and security personnel and even gardeners and chauffeurs, we are providing needed jobs and spreading the wealth. Besides, decent salaries and benefits are necessary to recruit good people to work in difficult situations. As for raising the salary level of national co-workers to a level similar to our own, would not that skew the local economy and reduce the amount of money available for other parts of our aid projects?

These are difficult problems and I am not sure that there is one solution for all of us. International organizations that support expatriates in developing countries have to balance the need of making their assistance money go as far as possible with the need of attracting good people to fill positions. Expatriates also have a balancing act to do. They have to balance their need for comfort, security, good education, and fairness to their families with the need to fit in and identify with the people whom they serve. Moderation, or finding a middle way, is how many philosophers define virtue. In truth, doing good is often a balancing act!

## *HOW ARE WE DOING IN MAKING THE WORLD A BETTER PLACE?*

There are therefore many challenges to us as individuals and to our organizations and nations as we try to do good internationally. In recent decades, many billions of dollars have been spent in international aid to developing countries and tens of thousands of technicians, diplomats, and others have been sent abroad to help. Is all of this help making any real difference?

The answer depends, of course, on whether one has the tendency to see a glass as half full or half empty. As we all know, there is still a tremendous amount of suffering in the world, and our countries and our organizations have wasted much money and effort. Wars, terror, natural disasters, pollution, AIDS and other diseases are causing social havoc and immense individual pain. Poor governance, corruption, prejudice, greed, and egotism cause it as well. Grinding poverty still chains millions in despair.

Yet, despite these enormous problems, much progress has also been made in the last few decades. The cold war has ended, and there is hope and excitement among many persons involved in some way in world economic and social development. It is an exhilarating time because in so many parts of the world the quality of life for people is actually improving. We can see this improvement in world health, economic, and social statistics, but we can sense it even more as we personally revisit places in Asia, South America, and Africa where we once lived or traveled decades ago. Things really do seem to be getting better in most places.

Science has played an important role in this improvement by developing effective medicines, efficient technologies, resistant strains of seeds, and new techniques to better people's lives. New levels of private, corporate, and governmental generosity have assisted in the spread of the benefits of these discoveries and technologies. Micro-loans have jump-started small businesses that have improved the lives of millions of people. Globalization has played an important part as well by establishing new common rules, reducing barriers, increasing trade, and sharing employment opportunities. The advancement of human rights has allowed people more freedom and access to jobs and services and better wages. Language learning, travel, and especially the internet have facilitated communication and understanding between peoples, and more and more people of different nations are visiting, studying, and working in other countries. Cell phones have made it possible for poor people in rural areas in developed and developing countries to communicate with each other and to become integrated into the life of their nations. Increased transparency and democracy are improving governance and accountability. Lobbying and education are making people more aware of the need of protecting our fragile environment and providing sustainable sources of healthy food and pure water.

So, while we are a long way yet from the kingdom of God on earth, and danger lurks around many corners, I think it is fair to say that many things are improving worldwide, and that yes, with God's help, we have made progress in making the world a better place. My hope and prayer is that he will continue to lead each of us so that we can complete the good works that he has prepared in advance for us to do. It is an exciting time to be alive and involved.

# CHAPTER 16
## *HOPE*

It is on this note of hope that I end this little book on what it means to me to be good and do good. In a relatively few pages, we have covered quite a lot of ground.

In the book, I have discussed many of the intellectual and practical difficulties we face in our feeble attempts to put into practice what I consider the master plan for a good and fruitful life—the admonition of Jesus to love God with all our being and to love others as we love ourselves. We have looked at what these commandments might mean and how we can get better at obeying them. We have seen how the love of God is the source, the motor, and the goal of a Christian's efforts to be and do good, and we have also considered how we can prepare ourselves to be co-workers with God in doing good deeds. Lastly, we have discussed some of the issues that we face and opportunities that we have to do good individually and in cooperation with others.

In some ways, this is a peculiar book dealing as it does with both religious belief and practical questions related to doing good locally and internationally. However, in doing good, all of these areas are intimately connected and therefore must be examined.

As I now come to the end of the book, I am glad that I wrote it, for it has helped me to understand a little better my own motivations, weaknesses, and struggles as I try to know God better and to be used by him to serve others in useful ways. Writing it has reminded me of concrete methods that I can use to keep my focus on God and on others and on the things that really matter in my own spiritual and ethical growth. It has also revealed to me how far I have yet to go! (My wife, children, and friends have not noticed any particular progress that I have made in becoming a better person during the writing process.)

While I am glad that I wrote the book for my own benefit, I must admit that I am also disappointed in it. I fear that it might not be as helpful to you the reader as I had hoped it would be. I am concerned that non-Christians will be turned off by the book's strong Christian emphasis, and that some Christian readers may see it as not Christian enough with its to-do lists and emphasis on "works" and not "grace." I also fear that international economic development experts may find it far too basic and without supporting statistics to be useful to them, and that other readers might wish that I had a more whimsical or inner-revealing writing style.

High aspirations and failure, however, seem to be our lot in this short life. We live our lives in fits and starts, sometimes advancing, but always falling far short of our ideals. We have great dreams, but we also have feet of clay. Our yearnings lift us up to God, but our egos and limitations keep us tightly chained to this world. We are called by God to work to free ourselves from these chains, but we know in the marrow of our bones that it is only his grace that will finally allow us to escape and fly upward to heaven. Only he can really change us and give us the wisdom to really be and do good and help others.

Thus, I end this book with the same disappointment in myself with which I began, but also with an increased trust in God and his mercy and with the conviction that one day "all will be well." I believe that in that day, good will totally conquer evil, life will win over death, joy over sorrow, compassion over selfishness, truth over falsehood, and mercy over justice. In that day you and I, and all of our brothers and sisters, will be transformed by God into the good people that we were meant to be—joyful citizens of his kingdom that has finally come on earth. Then we will see clearly and no longer have to struggle to be and do good. Being and doing good will be part of our nature.

# PART IV
## *APPENDIX*

# APPENDIX 1
## *Why I choose a Christian map*

I am a follower of Jesus Christ for many reasons. One is that I was brought up in a Christian home and in a mostly Christian region of the world and so it was the natural thing to be. Another deeper reason, though, is that the Christian view of the world and of humankind rings true to me.

That is not to say that Christianity does not seem strange and at times illogical! How rational is it to think that the world was created out of nothing? That God became man? That this God-Man did all kinds of miracles from healing to controlling storms and walking on water? That this God-Man, who had all power, majesty, and wisdom, allowed himself to be humiliated and to suffer the most terrible of deaths, and that somehow that death freed us? That he came to life again after he was dead? That he promised to live in and guide those who are his followers? That he promised them eternal life together with him? None of this is very logical!

Not only does Jesus' life seem strange, but also so do some of his teachings, especially those gathered together in what we know as the "Sermon on the Mount." Everyone wants to be happy, and most of us chase after that elusive happiness through possessions, sex, power, comfort, praise, and winning at whatever we try. However, Jesus teaches us that these are the wrong places in which to look for happiness. The happiness we find in those things is only momentary pleasure, and not the lasting joy that we really crave. He tells us that real happiness, the kind of peaceful joy that lasts and is there even in pain and change, is not to be found in riches, self-satisfaction, and pride, but in poverty of spirit. He tells us that true joy is not to be found in celebrating our achievements, but in mourning for our failures; not in illicit sex, but in purity of relationships; not in judgment of others, but in mercy;

not in aggressive, self-promoting behavior, but in peace-making and enduring insults for his sake. These are not our normal formulas for finding happiness! Yet even so, almost everyone, even people of other religions or no religion, exalts Jesus as a wise teacher; but very few people, including me, actually follow very closely what that wise man said.

So if much of Christianity seems so strange to me, and I am such a failure in translating Jesus' teachings into concrete deeds, why in the world would I call myself a Christian? Why do so many other people call themselves Christians? I suggest that one answer is that while at one level much of Christianity seems astounding, at a much deeper level, it all fits together and rings true. Christianity is a religion of paradoxes. It recognizes the huge importance of faith, but it is also rational. Indeed, many of the greatest rational minds in history have been convinced of the life, death, resurrection, and truth of the teachings of Jesus.

Personally, I find much wisdom and goodness in the teachings of Greek philosophy and of other religions. I also find much inspiration in the mystical and ethical lives of some of their saints. Still, I am convinced that the Christian view of Ultimate Reality is the correct one and that the simple instructions given by Jesus as to how we should live in order to attain lasting joy are the ones that we should try to follow. Here, briefly, are my reasons why:

First, I do not think that there is a separate Truth for science and for religion. Truth is Truth. In addition, Jesus says he is the Truth. We must use our reason and whatever reliable information we have to test this astounding claim and then come to the best decision we can about it, knowing that our decision, either affirming or denying the claim, will be based as much on faith as on reason.

Second, I believe in a Creator. While in my pride I do not want to be looked down on as unscientific and ignorant, the truth is that I cannot conceive of how this infinitely complex, orderly, exquisitely balanced, and beautiful world—from the smallest atom to the largest galaxy—came about by chance and unguided evolution. To believe that seems so unscientific and against reason to me, no matter how much time one gives for it all to happen. How can an eye or a brain or a strand of DNA come from nothing by chance and undirected evolution even in billions and billions of years? While I certainly believe that species adapt and evolve in some ways, I also believe that there has to be a Creator and Guider. To me, the "Big Bang" was an explosion with direction.

Third, I believe there is a shared, innate moral sense in all humans. I have lived in other countries and cultures, and while there are obviously huge differences in the way people look at and do things, there is remarkable unity in ethical standards. I believe that morality can be taught, but that there is also an innate code within each of us that guides us like a gyroscope telling us what is fair and unfair. It is like an instinct that our Creator instilled in us. No culture that I know of accepts as a universal good, murder, rape, robbery, and lying. The basic moral concept of "Do unto others as you would have them do unto you" is found in most religions in one form or another, as is the concept of fairness. Just as there are physical laws that undergird our existence, there are also moral laws that we infringe at our own risk.

Fourth, I believe that the Christian view of humankind is true. We are a mixture of goodness and evil, wheat and chaff, and that as much as we try, we cannot separate them on our own. On the one hand, we have been created in the image of God—our freedom, our creativity, our ability to love, our deep yearning for goodness and truth. As Augustine said, our hearts have no rest until they find rest in God in whose image we were created.

On the other hand, we are fallen creatures—victims of our egotism, our falseness, our ignorance, our physical and moral weakness. While it may be true that we have a moral code written on our hearts, it is also true that we are unable to follow it perfectly. We are not Rousseau's basically good creatures; nor to my way of thinking, Machiavelli's basically evil creatures either. We are created in the image of God, a little lower than the angels, but also all of us have sinned and our righteousness is as filthy rags.

Fifth, I believe that the Bible is an inspired book that tells the true story of God's revelation of himself through the history and writings of the Jewish people. Much more than the sacred books of other religions, the Bible is grounded in history and place and has been thoroughly investigated by historians, archeologists, textual scholars, and others and has stood up remarkably well against its detractors. It is an exceptional collection of books, written over many centuries by many different authors, that is unfailing in its realistic depiction of man in all his glory and failings, and its depiction of the nature and purpose of God.

Sixth, I believe that God is unknowable except through what he reveals about himself in scripture, in creation, in history, and in our own minds and spirits. Part of what he reveals about himself is that he is a Personal God who not only is the Designer and Creator of the cosmos, but is also the Source of all goodness, all truth, all power, all justice, all holiness, and all love. Sometimes we doubt this goodness and love of God because of the sickness, suffering, death, ugliness, and evil in the world. But while scripture never totally explains these imperfections and evils, we do know that usually they result from the wrong choices of humankind.

On the other hand, we see the grace and love of God everywhere as well. Look around at the beauty of nature that overwhelms us; breathe in the free air and drink the water we need to survive; marvel at the growth of the grains, fruits, and vegetables that sustain us. We experience his goodness in the beauty of the sunsets, the aroma of flowers, the sounds of rain and bird song, the touch of a friend's hand. "Taste and see that God is good," the Psalmist tells us. While the love and goodness of God is emphasized in all of creation and in the Bible, nowhere is it more clearly shown than in the words, life, and death of Jesus Christ for our sakes.

Seventh, I believe that Jesus is whom he said he is and did what the Bible said that he did. The accounts of him in the Bible can be traced to people who lived daily with him and were totally transformed by him. They were willing to die for the truth of his holiness, wisdom, redeeming sacrifice, real physical resurrection, and divinity even though all of this went totally against everything they had been taught and believed as Jews. I believe that Jesus is whom he and his disciples said he was because, otherwise, I would have to believe that he and his disciples were charlatans or insane, which they clearly were not.

I believe that Jesus is different from all other religious leaders. Moses, Confucius, Zoroaster, Buddha, Mohammed, and other historical religious leaders never claimed what Jesus claimed or were able to legitimize these claims by so many miracles, including his own physical resurrection. While I respect very much the teaching and lives of many of these other leaders, in my opinion they are in a different category. When Jesus asks his disciples if they will abandon him like others did because his teachings were difficult to understand and accept, Peter answers "Where else can we go?" For me, there is no one close to Jesus.

# APPENDIX 2
## *A CHECKLIST FOR GIVING*

This final appendix of this small book is a simple checklist of questions that perhaps can help us understand our motivations and giving habits and how we can learn to give better.

A. What are our honest feelings when requests are made to us?

1. Gratitude for an opportunity to serve?

2. Sense of superiority because we are being asked?

3. Thankfulness that we are not in the asker's shoes?

4. Compassion for the asker?

5. Contempt for the asker?

6. Discomfort at being put on the spot and confused as to what to say and do?

7. Guilt because we know we could answer the need, but we do not?

B. What are some of the policies that guide our giving?

1. Ego giving: We do not give unless it benefits us as well.

2. Free giving: We give to all who ask of us, without judgment.

3. Emotional giving: We give according to our emotions at the moment.

4. Rational giving: We ask ourselves questions like: How will our giving help or hurt the recipient in the short and long run? How will our giving to the recipient help or hurt others in the short and long run? How much can I afford to give in view of my other responsibilities? What is the most effective, efficient, and respectful way to give?

5. Duty giving: We give to those toward whom we feel responsibility, starting with ourselves, our families, and those organizations with which we are connected (like our schools and churches).

C. What are some reasons we have for not giving even when we have the resources?

1. We do not give to individuals, only to organizations (or vice versa).

2. We only give to organizations with which we are connected.

3. We only give if we can get a tax receipt.

4. We do not give over the phone.

5. We do not give to able-bodied people who can work.

6. We do not give to people whom we think are lying or manipulating us.

7. We do not give to people whom we think will use our gifts for drink or drugs.

8.   We do not give to children so they will not get into a bad habit of begging (unless they are selling things to raise money for a good cause or are children of friends).

D. What are the general criteria that guide our responses when asked for a gift?

1.   We do not have a policy or plan. We wing it.

2.   We do have a policy. We have thought things through.

3.   We try to listen to God's guidance at the moment.

## HOW CAN WE DO BETTER AT GIVING?

If we want to give to others, then it is useful to think through a giving plan so as we are not driven only by momentary emotions. The following are a few points to consider:

1.   Have a mission. What types of causes and people would we like to promote?

2.   Have principles to guide us in our giving: Here are just a few:

a.   Preserve the dignity of all concerned;

b.   Seek effective solutions—that really work;

c.   Seek efficient solutions—that use up the least resources possible and are still effective;

d.   Seek win-win solutions (benefiting the most people, even ourselves);

e.   Seek sustainability solutions (so that our gifts help a person or an organization become as self-sufficient as possible).

f. Follow Biblical injunctions about whom we should serve and support.

g. Follow the advice of wise persons, both alive and dead.

3. Have a budget for planned giving and for spontaneous giving. (How much of our income do we want to give? How much for planned and unplanned requests that are made to us?)

4. Have a system for evaluating an unplanned request:

   a. Where does the problem fall within our obligation zone?

      - Immediate family?
      - Other assumed responsibilities (job, organization, our word)?
      - Community responsibilities (friends, neighbors, etc.)?
      - Causes we believe in?

   b. Do we understand how our gift will be used to alleviate the problem and if there are any negative side effects our giving might have?

   c. What type of other help besides money can we give?

   d. What is the best alternative in this case?

      - Leave alone?
      - Lobbying and networking—Get others to help?
      - Advice and training?
      - Material—equipment, supplies, etc?
      - Money?
      - Combination of the above?
      - Other?

CPSIA information can be obtained at www.ICGtesting.com
Printed in the USA
BVOW041831081211

277871BV00002B/7/P